BY DAWNA MARKOVA, PH.D.,
AND ANGIE McARTHUR

*Reconcilable Differences: Connecting in
a Disconnected World*

*I AM Smart: A Guide to Recognizing and Developing
Your Child's Natural Strengths*

*Collaborative Intelligence: Thinking with
People Who Think Differently*

BY DAWNA MARKOVA, PH.D.

Wide Open: On Living with Purpose and Passion

Spot of Grace: Remarkable Stories of How You Do Make a Difference

*The SMART Parenting Revolution: A Powerful New Approach
to Unlocking Your Child's Potential*

I Will Not Die an Unlived Life: Reclaiming Purpose and Passion

*Learning Unlimited: Using Homework to Engage
Your Child's Natural Style of Intelligence* (with Anne R. Powell)

Random Acts of Kindness (with the Editors of Conari Press)

Kids' Random Acts of Kindness
(with the Editors of Conari Press and Rosalynn Carter)

The Open Mind: Exploring the 6 Patterns of Natural Intelligence

An Unused Intelligence: Physical Thinking for 21st Century Leadership
(with Andy Brynov)

*No Enemies Within: A Creative Process for
Discovering What's Right About What's Wrong*

*How Your Child Is Smart: A Life-Changing Approach
to Learning* (with Anne R. Powell)

*The Art of the Possible: A Compassionate Approach to
Understanding the Way People Think, Learn & Communicate*

RECONCILABLE
DIFFERENCES

RECONCILABLE
DIFFERENCES

Connecting in a Disconnected World

DAWNA MARKOVA, PH.D.,
and ANGIE McARTHUR

SPIEGEL & GRAU
NEW YORK

Published in the United States by Spiegel & Grau,
an imprint of Random House,
a division of Penguin Random House LLC, New York.

SPIEGEL & GRAU and Design is a registered trademark
of Penguin Random House LLC.

LIBRARY OF CONGRESS CATALOGING-IN-PUBLICATION DATA

NAMES: Markova, Dawna, author. | McArthur, Angie, author.
TITLE: Reconcilable differences : connecting in a disconnected world /
Dawna Markova, Ph.D., and Angie McArthur.
DESCRIPTION: First edition. | New York : Spiegel & Grau, [2017] |
Includes bibliographical references and index.
IDENTIFIERS: LCCN 2016047878 | ISBN 9780812997071 (hardback) |
ISBN 9780812997088 (ebook)
SUBJECTS: LCSH: Interpersonal communication. | Interpersonal relations.
CLASSIFICATION: LCC BF637.C45 .M345 2018 | DDC 158.2—dc23
LC record available at https://lccn.loc.gov/2016047878

Printed in the United States of America on acid-free paper

randomhousebooks.com
spiegelandgrau.com

246897531

First Edition

Book design by Casey Hampton

Understanding the human mind will be the greatest scientific adventure of the twenty-first century. There's no more profound or worthy study than how we learn, think, understand, and communicate.

—Charles Vest, former president,
Massachusetts Institute of Technology

AUTHORS' NOTE

This book has grown out of many years of our individual and collective experience. And while stories and examples are based on actual events, many of the places, names, and specific details regarding individuals we have worked with have been changed. In addition, some of the stories are based on composites of several individuals.

CONTENTS

INTRODUCTION:

Navigating the Great Relational Divide   *xiii*

CHAPTER 1: HARDWIRED TO CONNECT   3

DISCOVERY ONE: **COMMUNICATE**

Different Ways of Communicating—Through the
Discovery of Mind Patterns   *17*

CHAPTER 2: MAPPING THE WAY YOU COMMUNICATE   *19*

CHAPTER 3: RECONCILING THE DIFFERENCES
IN THE WAYS WE COMMUNICATE   *52*

DISCOVERY TWO: **UNDERSTAND**

Different Ways of Understanding—Through the
Discovery of Thinking Talents   *73*

CHAPTER 4: MAPPING THE WAY YOU UNDERSTAND   *75*

CHAPTER 5: RECONCILING THE DIFFERENCES
IN THE WAYS WE UNDERSTAND   *97*

DISCOVERY THREE: **LEARN**

Different Ways of Learning—Through the
Discovery of Inquiry Styles   *119*

CHAPTER 6: MAPPING THE WAY YOU LEARN   *121*

CHAPTER 7: RECONCILING THE DIFFERENCES
IN THE WAYS WE LEARN   *138*

DISCOVERY FOUR: **TRUST**

Different Ways of Trusting—Through the
Discovery of Personal Narratives   *155*

CHAPTER 8: MAPPING THE WAY YOU TRUST   *157*

CHAPTER 9: RECONCILING THE DIFFERENCES
IN THE WAYS WE GROW TRUST   *175*

CHAPTER 10: GROWING FROM EACH OTHER   *187*

Appendix—Mind Pattern Pairs   *195*

Appreciations to the Possibilists   *217*

Bibliography   *219*

Index   *223*

INTRODUCTION:
NAVIGATING THE GREAT
RELATIONAL DIVIDE

Vanity runs, love digs.

—Gustave Thibon

The two of us have been digging in to reconcile the differences between us for fifteen years. What are we digging into? The thick, rich, confusing soil of the different ways we think, experience, and understand the world. It was clear within the first ten minutes of meeting that we are radically different. Put it this way: If the human brain is 95 percent water, Angie's is like a still mountain lake and Dawna's is like a bubbling geyser. Dawna makes direct eye contact and tells provocative stories. Angie, on the other hand, looks off into the distance and asks evocative questions.

As mother and daughter-in-law, love (or even liking each other) was not a given. In fact, just the opposite. We both loved the same man, but in two very different ways—as son and as husband. No law in the world could force us to turn toward each other. Mothers and daughters-in-law more often run from each other or, at best, tolerate each other rather than dig in.

Our clear differences have not, however, kept us apart or hindered our ability to work well together. A year after we met in

1996, our family started a consulting partnership. And in 2015, after two decades of teaching and learning what we came to call intellectual diversity with global leadership teams, we distilled the results of our digging and discovering into the ink of our first book together, *Collaborative Intelligence: Thinking with People Who Think Differently.*

Since we've had a tremendous amount at stake professionally, we have not been able to take the way we relate to each other for granted. Each of us had to sort through our cognitive differences as they arose, and decide which were "givens," nonnegotiable: Angie's love of early morning runs and Dawna's nocturnal biorhythm, for instance. We then assumed all the other differences were "workables"—preferences, styles, dispositions, and proclivities that we needed to dig into and work out. This required us to respect and maximize our differences. Angie's need to question an idea from many angles, for example, helped us expand our thinking when we got stuck. Dawna's ability to think in stories helped us find meaning in challenges we faced.

With every new dimension we added to our business, friendship, and family dynamics, we have had to learn new ways to connect, understand, and harmonize our very different styles and ways of thinking.

Digging in means searching rather than knowing. Digging in means wondering, exploring. What is important to her? What really matters to me? What does she need now? What do I? What pisses her off? What's the rope in the tumult of any storm that she can hold on to? Like two fervent golden retriever puppies after a bone, we have been tracking a scent. Thoreau said, "Gnaw at it, bury it, unearth it, and gnaw it still." Dig in. We sniffed and scratched. Our understanding of each other grew. The questions and discoveries took us deeper into the humus of what could be possible. They carried us to the decision to write this book together.

Clients and friends have openly asked us how we do it—how two women who are so very different can be so in sync. We have come to respect and recognize that each person possesses many kinds of intelligence, including rational and relational. The former divides information into discrete facts, processes, and logic. Try to use your *rational thinking* when relating to someone who thinks differently than you do. You'll find yourself overthinking, trying to figure out whether you should say this or that, be this way or that way, do this thing or that thing. No matter how smart you are, your mind can become like a frustrated kitten tangled in a ball of yarn. The more you try to unravel the mess, the worse it gets. You become lost in your limited capacity to know or grow or relate to the mystery of your uniquely different ways of thinking.

Relational intelligence, on the other hand, connects things, creates meaning, and offers understanding about how to relate one thing or person to another. Most of us have been schooled in rational intelligence, but have never had specific formal training to foster relational intelligence. This is the bone the two of us have been digging to discover for twenty years, the answer to our clients' and friends' questions about how we do it: We have grown and never stop growing our relational intelligence.

The more wonder and discovery that are present between you and another, the higher the chances will be of that special kind of intelligence growing. Think for a moment about what it's like to sing in harmony with another person. Each of you allows your voice to come forward, fall back, and then merge to create beautiful music. It can be the same when we relate. If you know how to discover it, there is a palpable energy, an intelligence between you that can facilitate each of you achieving far more together than you could alone.

When people want to cultivate skills and talents such as playing the piano, solving complex mathematical equations, or hitting home runs, they can draw inspiration from and model themselves after great artists, athletes, and respected thought leaders. But we don't have ways to do this relationally. Just think for a moment: Who were your relational role models? If you're like most of us, you modeled your relational habits after those who raised you, for better or worse.

But even if you had the most loving and compassionate Nobel Prize–level people as your parents, you still have been bombarded daily in politics, on reality shows, and on the nightly news with examples of how *not* to relate to someone who thinks differently and how to run from them as fast as you can. Who has modeled for you how to dig in? Who are the relational geniuses you've learned from and how did they practice?

Thirty years ago, Dawna first witnessed a relational genius in action:

> I was backstage about to speak to a crowd of several thousand about my first book, *The Art of the Possible*. I noticed another woman sitting in a red leather swivel chair reading *The Boston Globe* and sipping tea from a thick, white, steaming mug. She looked up and grinned at me in such a way that I was speechless. I felt totally recognized, and at the same time recognized her as Maya Angelou. Evidently, we were both going to give keynote speeches within the hour. A copy of *I Know Why the Caged Bird Sings* lay unopened next to her tea. She went back to *The Boston Globe* and since I had no idea what to say to the great lady, I tried to ignore her, pacing back and forth as I flipped through my stack of note cards to review the key points for my talk.
>
> Maya Angelou, on the other hand, flipped through the newspaper and did something that I thought very odd. She paused at several pages with photographs of a person on them, rested her left hand on her heart, and stayed like that for a few moments. Each time, her face lit up in a grin as if she held the moon in her mouth. When she had gone through the entire section, she thumbed back to the beginning, and started the process again; only this time as she paused at different photographs and placed her hand on her heart, she shook her head sadly.
>
> I couldn't resist asking her what she was doing.
>
> "I am practicing," she said. "Yes, this is my practice. At

first, all of these people seem very different from me. The first time I go through the photographs in the paper, I pause at the pictures of people who have done remarkable things—built skyscrapers or discovered a cure for a disease or negotiated a peace settlement—and I say to myself, Well, if I can recognize that in them, it must be in me somewhere too or else why would I even be intrigued? So I just wonder for a moment, What does that remind me of in myself that I'd like to grow?"

It took a minute for her words to really sink in, but when they began to sprout in my mind, I responded, "That's lovely. I get that. But then why, if you don't mind my asking, do you go through the paper a second time?"

She looked up at me from under her eyelashes and said, "That's the hardest part of the practice. The second time I scan for people who have murdered or raped or destroyed something precious. This time when I pause again in recognition, I say to myself, Oh yes, that's in me, too; there is a dormant dark part inside. How can I delve in to discover the need under that destructive behavior so I can find a positive way of meeting it before it erupts?"

Then she placed both of her palms gently on the newspaper and tilted her head as she explained, "You see, I am learning something from each of these people parading across the pages of *The Boston Globe,* Dr. Markova. Each of them is teaching me to meet some aspect of myself that I might have ignored otherwise. This is what makes the bird in my heart sing."

Maya Angelou's "practice" was to constantly dig in as she learned to reconcile the needs of all the different aspects of herself—the best and worst. It also prepared her to relate to the multitude of those she encountered outside of her heart's cage.

Have you ever found yourself "at odds" with someone you care about? Reconciling the differences between you and someone you care about requires a leap into the unknown. It's like the adventure of exploring a foreign country where you don't understand the culture or the language. The roads you travel may seem to be full of wrong turns and dead ends.

If you have decided that your only options are fighting, fleeing, or freezing, please know we have written this book for you. If you wage a daily battle with the voice inside your head about which one of the two of you is right and which is wrong, this book is for you. And lastly, if you find yourself constantly worried about what the other person thinks of you, this book offers a very different way of considering that question.

By the time you've finished the last page, we hope you'll discover that you've cast aside much of your skepticism, doubt, and anxiety about interacting with that person. We imagine you feeling quiet but unmistakable confidence when you are with them. Your breath will go deeper and your field of vision will be wider. Sure-footedly, you will know you are moving forward. You may or may not know where you are going or what will happen, but the landscape will feel wide open, and your desire to discover as much as you can about yourself and the other will feel like an adventure that is leading you, connecting you to yourself and the world around you.

In order to get there, you'll need to replace a few limiting principles with ones that will liberate your thinking.

CARDINAL RULES OF RECONCILING DIFFERENCES

1. You can't change the other person—even for his or her own good. You can, however, grow your capacity to relate to them, to dig in with them.
2. You can't *make* them love, respect, or even like you, unconditionally or any other way. You can, however, find a way to respect yourself and how you are relating to the other, no matter what.
3. You can't prove to the other person that your perspective,

needs, and way of doing things are right, or better than his or hers. You can, however, grow your ability to recognize, accept, and value each of your differences.

The Form of This Book

- The way each of you **communicates** most authentically. Understanding this about each other will help you connect and develop rapport.
- The way each of you most naturally **understands** something. This discovery will help you to feel more energized, individually and together.
- The way each of you **learns.** This discovery will help you to better appreciate each other's perspective and what is important to each of you.
- The way each of you **trusts.** This discovery will increase your capacity to create meaning and a positive future between you.

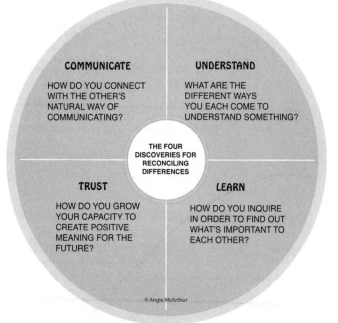

COMMUNICATE
HOW DO YOU CONNECT WITH THE OTHER'S NATURAL WAY OF COMMUNICATING?

UNDERSTAND
WHAT ARE THE DIFFERENT WAYS YOU EACH COME TO UNDERSTAND SOMETHING?

THE FOUR DISCOVERIES FOR RECONCILING DIFFERENCES

TRUST
HOW DO YOU GROW YOUR CAPACITY TO CREATE POSITIVE MEANING FOR THE FUTURE?

LEARN
HOW DO YOU INQUIRE IN ORDER TO FIND OUT WHAT'S IMPORTANT TO EACH OTHER?

© Angie McArthur

The first chapter in each section will help map your own process. The second will help you recognize and reconcile it with the other person's. In chapters 1 and 3, we introduce assessments that will help you discover differences in the way you and another person think, so that you can relate to each other more effectively. These tools also appeared in our previous book, *Collaborative Intelligence,* which focused on understanding intellectual diversity among teams and groups in a work setting. Practices throughout the book will help maximize the relevancy of these discoveries.

We offer this book to you as a guide for creating transformative moments and resonant times with a lover, family member, work partner, or friend where you each feel more authentic and alive. Let's begin by first understanding your own biases to relating to another and what you can do to overcome them. Dig in!

—Dawna and Angie

RECONCILABLE
DIFFERENCES

CHAPTER 1

Hardwired to Connect

Only connect!

—E. M. Forster

In times of challenge, most animals turn to some *place* for safety—a burrow, a rocky cave, a hole in a tree. But humans are unique in their tendency and need to turn toward one another for safety and growth; each of us has multiple regions in our brains devoted to empathizing, understanding, and relating to other people. We are not only Homo sapiens; we are also Homo empathicus, hardwired to relate, to connect, and to reconcile with others until the day we die.

Malcolm Gladwell, in his book *Outliers,* claims that it takes ten thousand hours of practice to become an expert at something. According to renowned neuropsychologist Matthew D. Lieberman, author of *Social: Why Our Brains Are Wired to Connect,* our brains naturally put those hours (and more) into becoming experts in the social world by the time we're ten. As Lieberman says, "Evolution has made a major bet on the value of our becoming social experts and in our being prepared at any moment to think and act socially." In theory, then, humans should all be relational experts. But most are not. Instead, members of our species continue to relate to one another in the same way over and over while expecting new results. This results in seemingly endless rejection, resentment, and retribution. What is the problem? Why is relating still so difficult? What *are* humans practicing during these ten thousand hours, and why aren't we experts yet?

In our experience, two significant factors interfere with inborn human relational capacity: lack of awareness of the power of attention, and the inability to relate to differences.

Reclaiming Your Attention

Our attention is the fuel that drives our lives. . . . No matter what people say about what they value, what matters is where they put their attention.

—ARIANNA HUFFINGTON

Buckminster Fuller, the renowned twentieth-century futurist and global thinker, described how making a small shift in the right place can have a huge impact on the effect we have and where we go. "Think of the *Queen Mary*," he wrote. "The whole ship goes by and then comes the rudder. And there's a tiny thing at the edge of the rudder called a trim-tab. It's a miniature rudder. Just moving the little trim-tab builds a low pressure that pulls the rudder [and the whole ship] around. Takes almost no effort at all."

Attention is the brain's trim-tab. It determines what you notice in the world, and how you notice it. If you don't claim and aim your attention, it will drag behind the ship of your mind, which will then be captured by the strongest current that flows around you.

As children, one of the first things you were taught is the importance of "paying" attention. You weren't given much choice about where your attention should be directed. Adults take charge of the trim-tab and say, "Pay attention. Look at me right now. Listen to me. You will be paying attention to geometry for the next forty-five minutes." Once you grow up, authority figures are no longer in charge of where you direct your attention, but who is? External signals from our bosses, colleagues, friends, children, lovers, as well as our electronic devices, now control the trim-tab. Author Jon Kabat-Zinn calls this our *collective* attention-deficit disorder.

There are three ways to take charge of your own trim-tab that will facilitate connecting with others:

Redirecting your attention from

- the noun "relationship" to the verb "relate"
- certainties to discoveries
- differences as difficulties to differences as resources.

RELATE, NOT *RELATIONSHIP*

Typically, people only stop to question *how* they are relating when they're in trouble—and even then speak of it as a doomed and static thing, a noun. "*Our relationship* is on the rocks," "We just don't click anymore," "*Our relationship* seems to have lost its fire."

In our experience, it is far more effective to direct your attention to the verb. How are you relating to that person? What effect are you having? If you don't judge yourself and instead stay curious, this wide and wondering state of attention will empower you to encounter the other person with a sense of discovery, in the same way Maya Angelou did as she studied *The Boston Globe.*

Consequently, we don't use the noun "relationship" throughout this book. As soon as you frame the interactions between you and another that way, you make it into an object, a photograph instead of a movie you are directing. Without realizing it, you relinquish your capacity to influence and navigate how you are creating the film. Consider the difference between saying to yourself, "This relationship sucks," and "The way I'm relating to this person sucks." The former produces a shrug. Your choices are to fight, flee, or freeze. In the latter, you are free to discover what adjustments you might make and to learn what is the best route toward the other person given the present circumstances.

DISCOVERY, NOT CERTAINTY

The second trim-tab of attention involves recognizing that relating to another person is an ongoing process of discovery, rather than following a memorized formula. If things were as simple as a formula, we would all have perfect marriages, children, and friendships. Instead, we need to reclaim wonder, which is no small thing. As Sherry Turkle points out in *Reclaiming Conversation: The Power of Talk in a Digital Age,* wonder is a rapidly disappearing commodity in our time and "not knowing" is no longer valued.

As soon as you've formed a fixed opinion of someone else or yourself, you've essentially killed them in your heart. If you want your relational capacity to grow, you have to learn to open your attention, accept uncertainty, and get comfortable with the confusion and groundlessness of not knowing.

In doing research for this book, the two of us realized we had to be willing to unlearn everything we thought we knew about each other and frequently get lost in wonder together. When you are lost, you can't just hold out your compass, find north, and then expect to continue in that direction forever. You may know someone well. You may think you know how to relate to them. But what if they go through a major health or personal crisis (or you do)? Perhaps you think you know how to relate to your children after eighteen years. When they go off to college, you discover that you have to start all over again, unless you want them to roll their eyes and sigh in exasperation when you try to speak to them in the way you've been doing for all those years. You will need to recalibrate by letting go of what you thought you knew about them, and start over in order to grow through that challenge.

Without this opening of your attention, no discovery is possible. Even if you have held them for your whole life, it still is necessary to unlearn, or suspend temporarily, the following certainties that keep your attention frozen and your mind closed:

- What you consider to be your own and the other person's deficits and faults
- The ways you believe the other person needs to change or improve
- The stories you are telling yourself about why you are right and the other person is wrong.

A Zen teaching describes this process as opening "the hand of thought." If you reflect for a moment on a time when you were disconnected from someone and not understanding them at all, you will most likely find that your mind was a lot like a fist. Recognizing this (without judging it) enables you to open your attention as you would open your clenched fingers. Voila! You are ready to reach and discover how connection can be possible.

DIFFERENCES, NOT DIFFICULTY

The third trim-tab of attention involves noticing how cognitive differences between us can be resources rather than deficits. What makes reconciling with a person who thinks differently so difficult? Is it really just clashing chemistry, timing, or personality? In our experience, the mental habit that creates relational divides and fragmentation is composed of four biases that keep us from connecting with others who think differently:

1. There is one right way to communicate.
2. There is one right way to understand.
3. There is one right way to learn.
4. There is one right way to trust.

Because we are not aware of these biases, we see those who communicate, think, inquire, and understand differently as "difficult people," adversaries, even enemies. In the past thirty years, there have been more than a hundred books published with titles like *Dealing with Difficult People, Coping with Difficult People, Dealing with People You Can't Stand, Powerful Phrases for Dealing with Difficult People* . . . The list goes on and on.

All of the books about "difficult" people reinforce your biases and shift your attention to how their differences are wrong. Consequently, most of what is currently called "relating" is really performing for others, maneuvering around them, categorizing, and trying to fix what's different between the two of you.

The underlying assumption in these books is that you will be much more effective if you find people who think just like you do. We disagree. The beauty of the human mind lies in how infinitely varied we all are, in our capacity to influence one another and use one another as resources.

During Dawna's experience in private practice as a psychotherapist, she observed these biases diminishing people's relational capacities:

> I sat hour after hour in my cozy office and listened to people struggling to reconcile with the differences between them and the significant others in their lives. They got caught in the habitual morass of trying to figure out who was to blame and who was the more difficult person. Without knowing it, they had been culturally directed to search for pathology, to ask, "Who is the crazy one here? What is wrong with my spouse? Why can't my brother see things the way I do? Why can't my kid pay attention to me?"
>
> Most people were searching for someone who was just like them, assuming that connection and understanding would happen organically if they had a lot in common. A point would always seem to arise, however, when what they began to notice was the other person's differences. "Why is this person so difficult?" I heard again and again. "He's my brother and we had

the same upbringing, so why can't we get along better?" It became obvious to me that "difficult" meant "different," and that "different" would come to mean "disrespected." That underlying disrespect gave way to a refusal to see another person or oneself in a new way. Biases locked them in the prison cell of their own certainty.

Uncovering Your Own Bias

To begin the process of reconciling the differences between you and someone with whom you're having trouble, you need to start with the consideration of what, exactly, might be making it difficult for you to relate to them.

Bring to mind a friend, a family member, or a colleague with whom you struggle. Think about what makes it difficult for you to connect with this person. Is she too loud? Unresponsive? Does she complain about everything? By becoming aware specifically of what it is that you take issue with about this person, you'll increase the possibility of moving beyond your own biases.

The following is a simple inventory of twenty-five characteristics that commonly annoy people about one another. Being as truthful as possible with yourself, note which of the statements apply to your "difficult" person:

1. They are spaced out and appear distracted.
2. They don't speak up enough.
3. You are confused by what they say.
4. You can't get a word in edgewise.
5. They sound wishy-washy.
6. They are difficult to communicate with.
7. They are impatient.
8. They are stuck in the past.
9. They are unrealistic.

10. They exaggerate.
11. They complain about fairness.
12. They are preachy.
13. They are always looking to fix you.
14. They don't support your vitality.
15. They point to what is wrong, criticizing and naming how it should be fixed.
16. They cross-examine, are skeptical, and want facts and data to justify things.
17. They ask questions that are scattered, unrelated, and indecisive.
18. They prompt questions with an emotion: "Don't you feel angry when . . . ?"
19. They do not recognize what's important to you.
20. They are very concerned with how they appear to others.
21. They see effort as fruitless: "Why bother?"
22. They don't ask for help and if help is offered they refuse it.
23. They need to be right and frequently blame others.
24. They do not support growth.
25. They can't seem to let go of opinions.

Even though you chose characteristics about the other person that you feel make it difficult for you to relate to them, what you selected also reveals your own biases that are limiting your connection: about the *right* way to communicate, the *right* way to understand, the *right* way to learn or ask questions, and the *right* way to grow trust. Indeed, if you feel that statements 1–6 describe your "difficult person," this reveals your bias about the *right* way to communicate. Statements 7–14 point to your bias around the *right* way to understand. Statements 15–20 point out your bias about the *right* way to learn. And statements 21–25 reveal your bias about the *right* way to grow trust. You may discover that you have one strong bias or several. There is no right or wrong; if you have more biases then there is only more for you to discover.

Think of these four biases as quadrants on a wheel.

We have divided this book into four corresponding sections. If you're able to identify which quadrant is most relevant for you, you may want to start with that section of this book. But working through all the biases will transform them into discoveries that enable reconciliation of differences.

The Voyage of Discovery

Tell me to what you pay attention and I will tell you who you are.
                                        —JOSÉ ORTEGA Y GASSET

There are several definitions of the word "reconcile" in the dictionary, and if we asked ten people, we'd surely get even more interpretations, so let's be clear about which of these the two of us are choosing: When you are reconciling with a person, you are recognizing the value of each of their cognitive differences. You are adjusting the way you think about a situation or an idea that is opposed to the way the other person is thinking about it. The two perspectives can exist together. And as long as we are defining things, when we say "recognize," we are referring to the Latin derivation of the word, which means "knowing again, as if for the first time." Thus as you move through the four discoveries of this book, you will be traveling through familiar landscapes, but seeing them with new eyes. You will be coming to know yourself and the other person in a whole new way.

When your mind is in this state of discovery with another, there is a vital relational energy that fills the space between you, enabling you to find possibilities that were previously overlooked. Lest you think this is ethereal, Angie had a practical experience in a drawing workshop that should make it more concrete:

> I was shown a picture of two people on a park bench. The instructor told me that rather than focusing my attention on the individual people, I should instead study and draw the shape of the space between them. In art, this is called the "negative space." At first, I couldn't stop looking at the people, but when I opened my attention beyond my biases of the two separate figures I thought I was supposed to draw, my awareness popped, and suddenly what was between them became alive and fascinating. I found myself in awe of new shapes, colors, and textures that were easy to draw on my own blank paper. Two human beings emerged even though I had drawn only the space between them.
>
> This is exactly what it feels like when you are reconciling the differences that you once perceived as difficulties. New possibilities emerge between you, along with a palpable energy, an intelligence that can facilitate each of you achieving far more together than you could alone. This vitality is what some people refer to when they use the expression "1 + 1 = 3."
>
> I used to believe the popular notion that this interconnection happens by chemistry, accident, or luck. But the past two decades of loving adventure with my husband, with Dawna, with dear family and close friends, has shown me that reconcil-

ing the differences between you and another helps you discover how to make choices that grow you both more alive.

Reconciling differences is an art form, but underlying the art are the four discoveries. In the next chapter you'll dig into the first by mapping your own communication style and then go on to recognizing another's in order to develop rapport.

RECLAIMING WONDER

Jiddu Krishnamurti, an Indian philosopher and spiritual teacher, put it this way: "When the mind is still, tranquil, listening, not seeking any answer or any solution . . . it is only then that there can be a regeneration, because the mind is capable of perceiving what is true." In this hypervigilant, know-it-all world it can be incredibly challenging to quiet your mind and to let go of everything you think you know about a beloved, a friend, a sibling, a child, and direct your attention toward what you don't know. But this is something we must work toward, because it is the most essential first step we can take toward relating.

PRACTICE: RECLAIMING YOUR ATTENTION

The following practice is an exquisitely simple and elegant way of taking charge of your attention. It helps you find sanity in the crazy moments of life. It can slow you down and bring awareness back into your body, where you can connect with your own internal state of mind—your thoughts, emotions, and needs in the present moment. From this centered place, you can relate more effectively to someone else.

- *Choose any sense: Notice what you feel in your body, hear, or see around you. For one minute write or describe out loud what you are experiencing.*

- *Include just the information your senses give you, without thoughts, comparisons, or opinions.*
- *For the next full minute, shift to another sense and describe it as above.*
- *For one more full minute, shift to a third sense and describe that one as above.*

Example: "Right now, I am seeing the birch tree outside my window move slightly in the wind. I see pollen and new fuzzy buds on the tips of branches. I see a red bird land on the grass and turn its head. I feel my fingers type and each of the keys spring back. I feel my butt pressing into the seat of the chair. I feel my neck tensing as I tilt my head back. I feel thirsty.

"I hear creaks in the walls of this old house. I hear the inhale of my breath. I hear the clicking of my keys. I hear music playing from my computer."

PRACTICE: THE MÖBIUS

The Möbius strip is a mathematical tool that we find very helpful as a model for discovering where your attention is and how it shifts when you relate. You will need a sheet of letter-sized paper and a pair of scissors. Hold your sheet of paper lengthwise and cut a two-inch strip down its side. Imagine that your strip represents the relational intelligence that you, like all humans, were born with.

1. *One side of the strip represents your awareness of yourself, and the other side your awareness of someone you care about. When you were an infant, you made no distinction between these two worlds. They were connected in your mind. As you grew, you were taught to differentiate between them, and to keep them separate.*

By adolescence, this strip had become a protective wall that separated the attention focused on your inner reality from the attention you focused on others. Bring the two ends together and tape them into a circle. This represents the way you were taught to build this protective wall around your inner life, putting all others on the outside.

2. Now, let's explore how you can shift to a discovery mindset by shifting where you focus your attention. Untape the ends of the strip and twist it once, reconnecting it into what is called a Möbius strip.

3. Trace your finger around the loop starting with the inside, where you discover what's important to you and what you think, feel, and need. As you continue tracing your finger, your attention will eventually come to a turning point, where attention begins to move to the other person. It is here that you can pause to discover the specific ways the other person communicates, thinks, inquires, and understands. It is also here that you can wonder, What's the quality of relating between us like right now? What effect am I having on him or her? What do I want it to be? What does he or she want it to be?

Discovery One:

COMMUNICATE

Different Ways of Communicating—
Through the Discovery of Mind Patterns

CHAPTER 2

Mapping the Way
You Communicate

It's not what we don't know that holds us back; it's what we do know that isn't so.

—Peter Senge

Reconciling differences presumes possibility. When the two of us enter a room, our first impulse is to search for ways to increase the synergy among the people who are in it. Neither of us is an optimist or a pessimist. Rather we are flagrant "possibilists." In any rift between two people, the key question that we are thinking is, What can be possible here?

The reason most people begin relating optimistically to another and then turn pessimistic is that they assume all humans do and should communicate in the same way. When they bump up against a difference, they shrug, chalking up dissension to personality or an intractable trait: "My husband takes up all the airspace. That's just the way he is. He talks and talks and won't listen to a word I've said."

"Whenever I try to get through to my daughter about something really important, she stares out the window, ignoring my perspective. She's done this since she was little. What's the point of trying?"

"I'm really attracted to this guy, but he just can't say how he feels. He tells me this is just how he is and I have to love him or leave him."

Do any of these communication breakdowns seem familiar to you? We have good news for you: Instead of being constantly frustrated by another person, reconciliation may hide in the differences between how each of you communicates. This discovery centers on how each person uniquely moves from one state of attention to another to express and receive information—what we call your mind pattern. In the last chapter we noticed where your attention goes and how to begin to redirect it. Now we move on to noticing how you can shift into different attentional states. Discovering that Dawna needs to talk in order to sort ideas, but Angie needs to go away and write, keeps the two of us from constantly wounding each other with words and silences. Nothing has helped us navigate our differences more, and create and maintain a loving respectful connection, than discovering the information in this chapter.

States of Attention

In Western cultures it's common to interject when a conversation has gone quiet, to jump in and help the other person—as if confusion is a sickness needing to be quickly cured—when they look pensive or lost in thought. However, being lost in thought is a state of attention where your mind is wide open, generating insights or ideas. In fact, this state of attention enables your brain to sort through information and digest it.

As your brain processes thoughts your attention moves through three different brain wave states: beta, alpha, and theta. The renowned psychiatrist Milton Erickson, M.D., called these three conscious, subconscious, and unconscious. We use the terms "focused," "sorting," and "open."

1. FOCUSED ATTENTION

This is the conscious state of mind when your brain produces more beta waves. Your thoughts become certain, and form into solid beliefs, like ice cubes. Your thoughts are very directed, and you are concentrating on what is in front of you: your computer screen, the other person's voice, the hammer in your hand. This is the state of attention best suited for:

- Concentrating on accomplishing tasks
- Converging on decisions
- Attending to details and timelines.

2. SORTING ATTENTION

This describes the subconscious state of mind where your brain produces more alpha waves. Your thoughts wander back and forth sorting through information, comparing one thing to another. You may experience this as confusion, or weighing two options, such as, "On the one hand . . . but on the other hand . . ." The ice cube of certainty melts and becomes more fluid. In this state of attention you are:

- Trying to understand
- Digesting information or experiences
- Thinking through confusion
- Weighing two choices.

3. OPEN ATTENTION

This is an unconscious state of mind where your brain is producing more theta waves. Your thoughts are very wide and internal, as in a daydream. Thoughts are like ice cubes that melted and have become as dispersed as steam. In this state you are:

- Highly sensitive to particular sounds, looks, or feelings
- Easily distracted and likely to forget certain details such

as proper nouns, the exact way something looked, the
specific way something felt, or what you did
- Imagining possibilities and new ways to approach old
problems
- Exploring different options by seeing things in a new way
- Associating to past experiences, stories, and people. "Oh,
that reminds me of this."

You may have experienced this open state while driving on the
highway at night—you pass by exit 15, and then suddenly find
yourself at exit 18, unaware of passing exits 16 and 17. Your attention has shifted from the cars around you, to a song on the
radio, to your own internal thoughts. But what has, in fact, happened is that your thoughts were shifting form, shifting from focused to sorting to open attention.

This state is where ingenuity can arise, new possibilities can be
imagined, and ruptured relationships can be repaired. Open attention is so crucial to our survival that our brains are structured
disproportionately in favor of it. Approximately 4 percent of a
person's neurological system is dedicated to conscious thought,
while 96 percent is dedicated to the unconscious state of attention.
You probably haven't learned to recognize this state of mind as a
valid type of thinking. But your mind *is* working without your
conscious awareness; it's just in an effortless state, making connections and thinking relationally.

You shift between these three states all the time with or without
awareness and each is relevant to communication. Together they
form a kind of "mental metabolism," where your mind is taking
in information, digesting it, rearranging it into new patterns and
ideas, eliminating and expressing it. Without recognizing them
you get caught in your biases. For example, you might misinterpret someone shifting into an open state of attention as being
bored with you.

Recognizing different states of attention in yourself and others
will help you avoid breakdowns in communication; you'll also

deepen respect and more easily develop rapport. For example, if someone is staring out the window, rather than misreading their distraction as being bored or not caring, you will instead now recognize that they are in a state of open attention. Or, if your mind is really focused, you will know to ask for time to complete what you are doing before turning toward someone who wants your attention.

There are two fascinating things about this. The first is that you can learn how to intentionally shift from one state of attention to another. The second is that different people are triggered into these states of attention in different ways.

Languages of Thought

Different experiences and events trigger people into focused, sorting, and open states, depending on how their brains are wired. It might seem as if these shifts in attention just happen automatically, but there are actually three triggers: auditory, which refers to talking and listening; kinesthetic, which refers to movements and feelings; and visual, which encompasses experiences like looking at something, reading, or writing. We call these three categories the languages of thought. What's notable is that every person will respond to these triggers differently.

Auditory input—listening and talking—triggers a focused state in some people. Think of someone you know who is quick with his or her words, and highly articulate—the more they talk, the more energized they become. That person responds to auditory input. For others, auditory input triggers a sorting state of attention. Think of someone you know who likes to dialogue back and forth, talking things through. For still others, auditory input triggers an open state of attention, putting them into a questioning or daydreaming frame of mind. Someone like this may come across as quiet, take longer to find their words, and be more apt to ask questions and pause to listen for a while before speaking.

Visual information likewise generates a focused state for people who are able to manage a large amount of visual detail at once. For others, visual detail may trigger a sorting state of mind where they are able to see things from two perspectives at once. For others, visual input can trigger an open state, causing them to appear spaced out or lost in trance.

Kinesthetic input, which includes touch and physical movement, will trigger some people to be focused and alert; for others, movement will trigger sorting attention. For a third group of people, kinesthetic will space them out, and these people may be especially sensitive to physical touch.

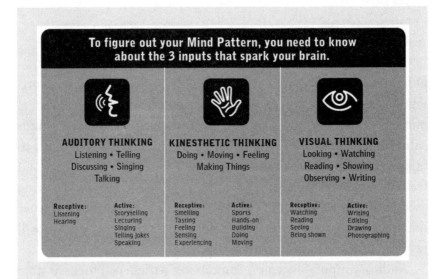

Recognizing Your Mind Pattern

You may have heard people refer to themselves as visual or auditory learners, but this kind of statement is an oversimplification; it really refers to only what triggers their focused state of attention. But what isn't recognized is that all states of attention—focused, sorting, and open—are necessary to think, learn, and communicate. Each is evoked by a different language of thought—auditory, kinesthetic, and visual. The three languages of thought and the three states of attention combine to create six unique mind patterns. By the time you reach puberty, your mind has habitually grooved into one of these 1-2-3 sequences.

Identifying your mind pattern—the sequence that your brain uses to process information—will increase your self-awareness and ultimately make your communication with others more effective. And it's simpler than you might think. It only requires that you pay closer attention to the effect on your state of attention that each of the three languages of thought has on you. For example, do visual details distract you or help you to focus? Do you speak in a detailed manner without hesitation? Or do you talk in metaphors and stories? At first this may all seem a bit inscrutable—we are challenging you to become more aware of things that you don't habitually notice. You have been using your mind like the automatic transmission of a car, unaware of the gears shifting. But we are asking you to start listening to the sounds of the engine as it turns.

The self-assessment map that follows will lead you to one of six mind patterns. Move through it like the game of "Hotter/Colder."

Step 1: Read through all three cards down the left side of the page (A1, V1, and K1). Choose the card that has the *most* characteristics that feel true for you. Any single characteristic in and of itself may not fit but what is significant is the *overall* card.

Step 2: Follow the arrow from the card you chose and then select one of the two cards to the right that most applies to you— K2, A2, and V2.

Step 3: Follow the arrow and look at the bottom of the card from step 2, and the map will direct you to the next particular card in the far right column: V3, K3, or A3.

Step 4: Read the chart of six possible mind pattern combinations. One of them will match each of the three choices you made in the map. This is your mind pattern: The first letter and sensory symbol represent what helps your mind focus, the second represents what helps you sort information, and the third represents what helps your mind open your attention.

STEP 1

Choose one of the cards below that seems most true for you, then proceed to the next step.

STEP 2

Choose which of the following two cards is most true for you.

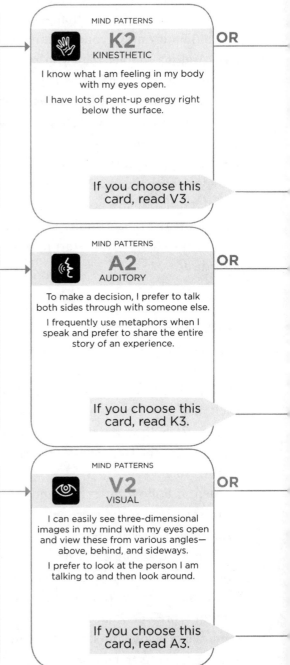

MIND PATTERNS

A1
AUDITORY

I'm comfortable talking to large groups of people, even without advance preparation.

I prefer to give verbal reports rather than do a visual presentation or make a model.

I naturally remember what's said in a conversation.

I speak without pause (no "um"s) and use precise language.

Words flow out easily in logical order without thinking about it.

I can multitask auditorily: I can talk with one person and listen to somone else in the background at the same time.

I tend to be critical of how things are said.

MIND PATTERNS

V1
VISUAL

The first thing I recall of a person or place is the way something or someone looked.

I'd prefer to write a report rather than do an oral presentation or make a model.

The best way for me to organize is to make a list.

I like to make direct and steady eye contact with the person I'm talking to.

I'm highly aware of the way I look to other people.

I can multitask visually: I can read and watch TV at the same time.

I tend to be critical of how things look.

MIND PATTERNS

K1
KINESTHETIC

I prefer to be on my feet or moving around. A stand-up desk would really help me.

I prefer to share an experience or make a model as a presentation.

The best way for me to organize is by making piles.

I can easily recall what I did and the physical sensations of an experience.

My natural preference is to start hands-on and experiment by doing.

I can multitask kinesthetically: I can do two or three things at the same time.

I tend to be critical of how things are done.

MIND PATTERNS

K2
KINESTHETIC

I know what I am feeling in my body with my eyes open.

I have lots of pent-up energy right below the surface.

If you choose this card, read V3.

OR

MIND PATTERNS

A2
AUDITORY

To make a decision, I prefer to talk both sides through with someone else.

I frequently use metaphors when I speak and prefer to share the entire story of an experience.

If you choose this card, read K3.

OR

MIND PATTERNS

V2
VISUAL

I can easily see three-dimensional images in my mind with my eyes open and view these from various angles—above, behind, and sideways.

I prefer to look at the person I am talking to and then look around.

If you choose this card, read A3.

OR

STEP 3

Read the card that your choice indicated in Step 2.

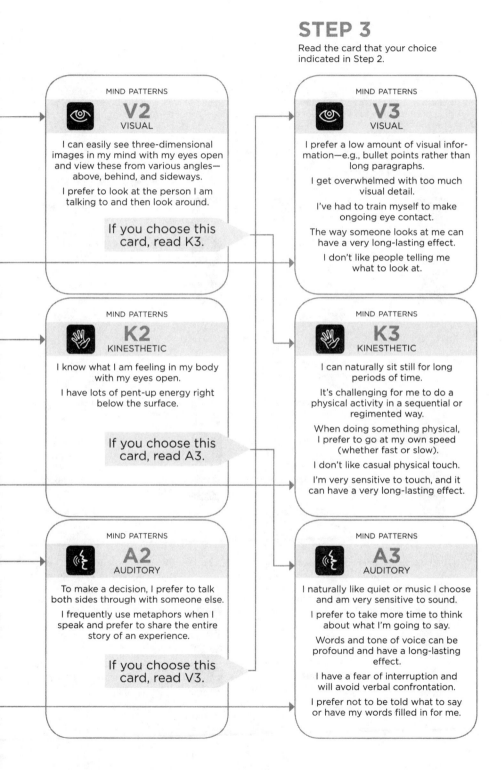

MIND PATTERNS

V2
VISUAL

I can easily see three-dimensional images in my mind with my eyes open and view these from various angles— above, behind, and sideways.

I prefer to look at the person I am talking to and then look around.

If you choose this card, read K3.

MIND PATTERNS

V3
VISUAL

I prefer a low amount of visual infor- mation—e.g., bullet points rather than long paragraphs.

I get overwhelmed with too much visual detail.

I've had to train myself to make ongoing eye contact.

The way someone looks at me can have a very long-lasting effect.

I don't like people telling me what to look at.

MIND PATTERNS

K2
KINESTHETIC

I know what I am feeling in my body with my eyes open.

I have lots of pent-up energy right below the surface.

If you choose this card, read A3.

MIND PATTERNS

K3
KINESTHETIC

I can naturally sit still for long periods of time.

It's challenging for me to do a physical activity in a sequential or regimented way.

When doing something physical, I prefer to go at my own speed (whether fast or slow).

I don't like casual physical touch.

I'm very sensitive to touch, and it can have a very long-lasting effect.

MIND PATTERNS

A2
AUDITORY

To make a decision, I prefer to talk both sides through with someone else.

I frequently use metaphors when I speak and prefer to share the entire story of an experience.

If you choose this card, read V3.

MIND PATTERNS

A3
AUDITORY

I naturally like quiet or music I choose and am very sensitive to sound.

I prefer to take more time to think about what I'm going to say.

Words and tone of voice can be profound and have a long-lasting effect.

I have a fear of interruption and will avoid verbal confrontation.

I prefer not to be told what to say or have my words filled in for me.

STEP 4

In the graphics below, find the mind pattern that you chose and proceed to the indicated page for a more detailed description.

If this description does not seem like you, revisit your previous choices or refer to the mind-pattern chart on page 24, and see if there is a mind pattern that fits you better. It is helpful to read through all six patterns and then observe yourself over the next couple of days with this context in mind. This will give you insight into which sequence supports your mind to focus, sort, and open most effectively.

Now that you've explored the self-assessment map, you may have a sense of the mind pattern that fits best for you. If your mind is still churning possibilities, reading through the following snapshots of each pattern may be clarifying. They were developed over thirty years with input from thousands of people who attended our workshops. The sketches were created by a group of counselors, therapists, and social workers during a four-day seminar in Rhode Island. They distill many aspects of each mind pattern into one representative message.

You are not looking for a pigeonhole. You are just discovering what helps you focus, sort, and open your attention. Keep in mind that mind patterns do *not* describe personality or gender, although the characteristics of a person's mind pattern are often misconstrued in this way. If, over time, the mind pattern that you selected does not seem to fit, you may want to read through the other patterns and see if another is more accurate. Some people recognize their pattern immediately. Others need to observe themselves in this new way over time, until they find an accurate fit.

MIND PATTERN MAPS

VAK—Visually Focuses, Auditorily Sorts, Kinesthetically Opens

Visual, Auditory, and Kinesthetic VAK PATTERN			
V1	👁	FOCUSED THINKING	To Trigger Concentration: VISUAL
A2	👂	SORTING THINKING	To Trigger Sorting: AUDITORY
K3	✋	OPEN THINKING	To Trigger Imagination: KINESTHETIC

To avoid being boring, often I embellished my tales with color-fully concocted extravagant elaborations. . . . By now, I believe whatever I make up about myself.

—SHELDON KOPP, twentieth-century

psychotherapist and author

The VAK Snapshot

More than anything, you want to help others see things in a new way. You frequently "show and tell." You make a visual impression with the colorful, well-coordinated clothes you wear. Visual details are important. You habitually read anything in your view—including cereal boxes, billboards, novels.

You best become focused and alert by bringing your attention to visual details or writing something down. You best have insights by closing your eyes or looking away, then listening to sounds around you, and then feeling the overall sensations in your body while walking, driving, or taking a shower.

List making and taking notes are important ways of organizing information for you, though you may not need to go back and read them. You memorize by reading, writing, and then saying it out loud.

You speak persuasively, with a lot of feeling and energy behind your words. Hand gestures follow what you say to emphasize a point. You naturally teach and explain things, and love to tell stories that paint pictures with metaphors. You tend to use visual vocabulary when speaking: "see," "look," "colorful," "show," "bright," "I can see your point," "See you later."

You prefer back-and-forth dialogue as a way to think out loud with someone else in order to sort through options and reach clarity about what you really think.

Your emotions are written all over your face, but you may have to close your eyes to know how you are feeling in your body.

Touch is private for you. You tend to avoid a casual touch on the arm or hugs from people unless you know them well. Competitive sports with lots of physical contact may consequently be something you shy away from.

SKETCH: A MESSAGE FROM SOMEONE WHO USES THE
VAK MIND PATTERN

I've always been involved with a lot of paper. Books are important
to me. If someone comes into my house and reads the titles of my
books and magazines, they know a lot about me right away. That's
the part of me I want people to know. I collect things to read, so I
never run out.

I watch movies and TV a lot, but there are times I overdo it. I
consider myself a visual addict, because I sometimes choose
watching stories over the experience of real life.

When I am communicating well, I tell stories that make me feel
more alive and I bring out the other person with evocative images.
If there is a communication difficulty, I tend to ignore what I feel
in my body. I make a movie in my mind of who is right and who's
at fault and then verbally defend that story.

As far as physical affection goes, well, before you learn that
about me, we need to have many intimate conversations first.
What I will tell you is I like to hear positive things about how I look
to you, and talk awhile before I go any further.

VAK Characteristics

WHAT COMES NATURALLY?

- You instinctively teach or convince when you talk even if
  that isn't your intention.
- You make lists to organize.
- You have excellent visual recall—for faces, what someone
  was wearing, what something looked like.
- You can work at visual tasks for long periods of time.
- You're good at weaving stories that are inspiring or moti-
  vating to others.

WHAT HELPS YOU COMMUNICATE MOST EFFECTIVELY WITH ANOTHER?

- Give a headline before you launch into a story.
- Ask yourself what is the main point you want to convey. For example, "I'd like to tell you about a time when I was terrified to go in the ocean."
- If you find yourself trying to convince your listener, check in with questions to make sure they are following you. For example, "Are you with me on this?"
- If there's no time or interest in your stories or you are caught in a down-spiraling conversation, switch to an email, text, or write out/draw what you want to say.
- Getting up and walking around will help you recognize what you are feeling without getting flooded by your emotions.
- Your communication style leads you to inspire people with stories.

WHAT HELPS ANOTHER BEST COMMUNICATE WITH YOU?

- To connect well, you need as much eye contact as possible (for example, via webcam).
- To show you that they care, others should send emails, texts, or cards as frequently as possible to check in or schedule anything.
- To clear confusion, you like to arrange time to talk issues over.
- If there is a serious disagreement, you want to be invited to go for a walk to discuss it, or use a webcam and be encouraged to walk around.
- To teach you a physical task (exercise), others should show you first, then give you verbal instructions with a

metaphor. Keep your eye on the ball as if it was a gift coming to you.

VKA — Visually Focuses, Kinesthetically Sorts, Auditorily Opens

Visual, Kinesthetic, and Auditory VKA PATTERN		
V1	**FOCUSED THINKING**	To Trigger Concentration: **VISUAL**
K2	**SORTING THINKING**	To Trigger Sorting: **KINESTHETIC**
A3	**OPEN THINKING**	To Trigger Imagination: **AUDITORY**

The only true voyage of discovery . . . would be not to visit strange lands but to possess other eyes.

—Marcel Proust

The VKA Snapshot

People are struck right away by your empathetic energy. You seem to drink in the world through your eyes and feel what you see. You are visually meticulous, wanting clothes, possessions, and surroundings to fit an image you have created in your mind. You can't think well with visual clutter. You have an aptitude for proofreading and can design things in detail. You tend to depend on written reminders, lists, instructions, and directions to keep yourself well organized.

You focus best by bringing your attention to visual details or writing something down. You generate insights by closing your eyes or looking away, then feeling the overall sensations in your body, while listening to soothing music or noticing natural sounds.

You check out if others talk on and on, unless you take copious notes. It is easy for you to write down what you hear almost word for word. You easily remember what you've seen but may forget what you've heard. You recall people's faces, but may forget their names.

You have excellent eye-hand and eye-body coordination, learning best by watching a demonstration or reading the directions for a task and then experimenting in how to do it, without first being told. You memorize most easily by writing something repeatedly.

Usually you have a lot of wound-up physical energy, so activity is an important emotional and energetic outlet. You are interested in how everything from complex machines to the human body works and also have a highly developed empathetic sense of other people.

You often feel pulled in two directions and may vacillate before making up your mind. Direct experience seems to be your best teacher in sorting things out. If you can see and try out options, you can know what's right for you.

Although you listen deeply, you can be quiet and keep to yourself, especially in large groups. It is difficult for you to speak off the cuff, be asked specifics about what you've heard, or remember proper nouns.

You use lots of visual vocabulary such as "look," "see," "show," "imagine," "I can picture that," or "See you soon." You tend to communicate by naturally asking one question after another.

SKETCH: A MESSAGE FROM SOMEONE WHO USES THE VKA MIND PATTERN

I can feel the way things could be when I look at them. I love designing exterior and interior spaces. I hate verbal fights and arguments. I pull as far away as I can in my mind from someone who has a loud voice or sharp tone.

I feel what I see. Have I said that? I can almost always tell what others are feeling just by looking at them, but it is sometimes hard for me to differentiate between what I imagine they are feeling and what I perceive.

If I want to really hear something, I need to close my eyes. I don't like to be told what to do. Well, that's not exactly true; part of me likes rules and structure, and a secret part hates them. Walking makes it easier for me to talk. Words don't come easily to me.

VKA Characteristics

WHAT COMES NATURALLY?

- You have excellent eye-hand and eye-body coordination.
- You remember easily what you have seen or read.
- You can pick up the feelings and sensations being experienced by others around you.
- You have good spelling and proofreading ability.
- Your communication style is best used to maintain the connections between people.

WHAT HELPS YOU COMMUNICATE MOST EFFECTIVELY WITH ANOTHER?

- Use visual cues in PowerPoints or notes so that you don't have to worry about forgetting what you want to say.
- Moving while talking or listening will help you to concentrate on what others are saying.
- Most likely you are a good communicator one-on-one and in small groups. Try to get very clear about what you think by writing before you talk with others; you may find yourself being swayed by others' opinions and agreeing to something you really don't believe in.
- To speak in front of a large group, prepare visually in advance, move around, and draw on a whiteboard or use bullet points to keep you on track.

WHAT HELPS ANOTHER BEST COMMUNICATE WITH YOU?

- To connect well, you need as much eye contact as possible; use a webcam rather than a teleconference.

- To see that others care, you want to receive emails, texts, and surprise notes.
- To clear confusion, you want to receive an email, and then arrange to walk and talk it over if possible.
- If there is a serious disagreement, others should write you a text or email and invite you to go for a walk to discuss it, or use a webcam and encourage you to walk around. They should be aware that you are highly sensitive to tone of voice.
- To teach you a physical task or exercise, others should show you first, then let you experiment and ask questions about the details of what you've heard.

KAV—Kinesthetically Focuses, Auditorily Sorts, Visually Opens

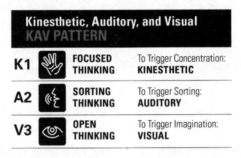

Kinesthetic, Auditory, and Visual KAV PATTERN			
K1		FOCUSED THINKING	To Trigger Concentration: KINESTHETIC
A2		SORTING THINKING	To Trigger Sorting: AUDITORY
V3		OPEN THINKING	To Trigger Imagination: VISUAL

Sometimes the skin seems to be the best listener, as it prickles and thrills, say to a sound or silence; or the fantasy, the imagination: how it bursts into inner pictures as it listens and then responds by pressing its language, its forms, into the listening clay.

—M. C. Richards

The KAV Snapshot

You are the one who "gets things done," prefers to be on your feet and in action rather than sitting at a desk. You generally have amazing physical stamina and do things in a logical fashion. You tend to be very present in your body, well coordinated, in perpetual motion, and a "natural" athlete who seems to have an endless supply of physical energy. You can access and verbalize body sensations in a specific, organized way, naming where your head hurts or which muscle in your leg is pulled. Physical comfort is quite important to you, as in choosing clothes by the right weight and texture, and furniture by how it functions. Your preference is to relate to the world first in some tangible way—by touching, tasting, smelling, or experiencing anything new with your hands or whole body.

You best become focused and alert by moving. You generate insights most effectively by being still, then listening to sounds around you, and then making a movie in your mind.

Touch comes naturally and easily for you and is an important way to connect; it is casual for you. It's not easy for someone else to read how you feel by looking at your face. Your body says it all by how you stand, move, or touch. When communicating, your hand gestures will precede your words, and you enjoy talking about what you've been doing, how you did it, and how it felt to do it. You use a lot of kinesthetic vocabulary—words and phrases that describe action or feeling, such as "getting a feel for," "How does that grab you?," or "I can't get a handle on it"; and you use kinesthetic metaphors when speaking: "Throw it fast and fierce like a bullet." You often want to convince others to do things your way. It helps you to sort things out by talking about them.

You look away from others because your eyes tend to be very sensitive, and you prefer to keep them averted (or wear sunglasses indoors), making occasional glances to check in with the person speaking. If required to "look" for too long, your eyes may glaze over. You can listen intently, making little or no eye contact at all, even while being busy doing something else.

You are deeply influenced by external visual images, and "nasty" looks that indicate judgment or criticism to you. On the other hand, smiles and looks of love and appreciation can also leave a lasting impression.

Writing can be laborious, but it can also be your art form, if you can do it at your own rhythm without too much criticism. You can be easily overwhelmed by too many visual details, and your preference is to take in a wide view so you can capture the whole picture of something with just a quick glance.

SKETCH: A MESSAGE FROM SOMEONE WHO USES THE KAV MIND PATTERN

Sitting still for long periods of time has always been torture to me and I avoid it whenever I can. Being in nature, sports, using my hands is always how I feel most authentic and real. If I don't move, my feelings can boil up to the surface as if I'm emotionally hemorrhaging. I am frequently labeled as ADHD, but when I'm doing, moving, or touching I have no problem focusing my attention. My mind comes alive when I can have an experience first, then talk about it, and lastly read or write about it.

I've always had a certain allegiance to and understanding of people who work with their hands—farmers, laborers, carpenters, waitresses, athletes, and many others who get lost in the shuffle.

When I'm communicating well, I know how I'm feeling and what I want, and I love helping people accomplish things together or learn how to do something. I'm good at recounting physical experiences I've had. When there's a communication difficulty, I tend to isolate myself so I don't explode. If you force me to look at you steadily, I may back away or even say something that pisses you off just to get some space. I love to be told how I make a difference, but please don't ask me to notice how you look.

KAV Characteristics

WHAT COMES NATURALLY?

- You have a great deal of physical stamina.
- You're a competent hands-on "doer," who prefers to be on your feet and in action.

- You do things in a logical and systematic manner. Your movements are strong, steady, direct, and detailed.
- You enjoy telling stories of what you've done, how you did it, and how it felt to do it.
- You're skilled at teaching people how to do things since translating action into words is easy.

WHAT HELPS YOU COMMUNICATE MOST EFFECTIVELY WITH ANOTHER?

- Give yourself permission to stand up, move around, or hold something in your hands.
- Whenever possible, walk and talk in nature or at least outdoors.
- Talk about what you are experiencing in your body and use questions to check in to make sure the other person is following you.
- If you feel caught in a down-spiraling conversation, explain that you need some space and time, and commit to when you will reengage.
- Your communication style inspires people to take action.

WHAT HELPS ANOTHER BEST COMMUNICATE WITH YOU?

- To connect well, you need movement, physical contact, or shared physical activity, rather than phone or email, whenever possible. The more live interaction the better.
- The most effective way for others to demonstrate that they care about you is through shared experiences, touch, talking about feelings, and ultimately making their caring visible in some simple way, such as a photo, poem, or significant object.
- To clear up confusion, request that others walk and talk issues over with you.

- If there is a serious disagreement, encourage others to go for a walk, in nature if possible, to discuss it rather than sitting face-to-face.
- It is important for you to sort things out verbally before arriving at understanding or convergence on outcome.
- In order for you to learn a new task from someone, have them talk you through it step-by-step while you do it. If they have to use visuals, ask for one or two simple diagrams. Explain that you prefer a low amount of visual input, and dislike detailed written instructions. Arrows or text that indicate sequence or action steps can be helpful.

KVA—Kinesthetically Focuses, Visually Sorts, Auditorily Opens

Kinesthetic, Visual, and Auditory KVA PATTERN			
K1		FOCUSED THINKING	To Trigger Concentration: KINESTHETIC
V2		SORTING THINKING	To Trigger Sorting: VISUAL
A3		OPEN THINKING	To Trigger Imagination: AUDITORY

The words or the language, as they are written or spoken, do not seem to play any role in my mechanism of thought. The psychical entities which seem to serve as elements in my thought are certain signs and more or less clear images which can be "voluntarily" reproduced and combined. . . . The above-mentioned elements are, in my case, of visual and some of muscular type. Conventional words or other signs have to be sought for laboriously only in a secondary stage.

—ALBERT EINSTEIN (quoted by
Jacques Hadamard), *Ideas and Opinions*

The KVA Snapshot

You are private, with a grounded physical presence, and seem to be surrounded by a deep silence. You have smooth, receptive energy and seem to be most alive when you are moving. You often are interested in seemingly diverse and dissimilar things—football and art, or photography and chemistry. You seem to have an intuitive sense of how everything fits together. What matters to you is living from a place of integrity.

You best become focused and alert by moving around and seeing the visual details of your surroundings, while asking yourself a question about what you need to do. You have your best insights when you first move or touch something, then look around, doodle, or draw things out, while listening to soothing sounds or basking in silence.

You prefer to be "doing" as much as possible, and tend to be a concrete learner. You acquire new physical skills with ease by doing and watching and then asking questions. You are very well organized and detailed in what you do. You have good eye-hand coordination, often like working with your hands, and are easily able to put things together, sometimes in very creative ways.

You are very aware of the specific sensations in your body. Since physical comfort is quite important to you, you may go to great lengths to find the right chair or the right position to sit in.

You feel things deeply, but it may be difficult for you to express it in words. When you are angry, you tend to withdraw rather than lash out. Touch usually comes naturally and easily.

Your eyes will glaze over if you listen to too many words, and you usually need to look away to find what you want to say. You have a three-dimensional way of making images, meaning you can see things from many perspectives with your eyes open.

Harsh or critical spoken phrases or tone of voice can echo in your mind for years. Speaking in front of groups can also be difficult unless you have visuals or hands-on cues to bridge the gap. You don't like to talk off the top of your head, and may freeze if pressured to speak.

You frequently use a lot of kinesthetic vocabulary, words that convey action or feelings, like "grab," "hold," "soft," or "move," and phrases like "That feels right," or "I'll be in touch soon."

SKETCH: A MESSAGE FROM SOMEONE WHO USES THE KVA MIND PATTERN

Moving helps me think and be comfortable—you might say I like to wonder and wander. People say I keep a lot hidden, but that's not really how it is. If I don't feel safe, I make myself invisible by blending in with the background. If I get mad at someone, it's easier for me to poke him or her than try to talk it out right away. When I am communicating well, I love to share the possibilities I see and ask questions.

I experiment visually by moving things around and then looking to see if it works. I'm inspired by visual beauty and symmetry.

For me to speak when there is a communication difficulty feels like jumping off a high cliff. I will shut down if others interrupt me or put words in my mouth. Silence or a question after I speak tells me you understand. Listening to music without words is meditative and calming for me.

KVA Characteristics

WHAT COMES NATURALLY?

- You can get things done logically and systematically, with lots of stamina.
- You can acquire new physical skills with ease.
- You're able to see things from many perspectives, including the validity of many sides of an issue.

- You can hear the whole of something, such as harmonies and themes.
- You have good eye-hand coordination and can create complex things in three dimensions.

WHAT HELPS YOU COMMUNICATE MOST EFFECTIVELY WITH ANOTHER?

- You need to feel safe and listened to in order to enter into meaningful conversation.
- The more you can be on your feet and have direct experiences with others, the better. For example, "Walk over here with me and let me show you what I mean."
- Be aware that other people aren't as verbally sensitive as you, and try not to take their tone of voice or phrasing personally.
- Whenever possible, communicate with others in writing—email, notes, and memos—especially if you want to express your feelings.
- Your communication style inspires people to act with integrity and vision.

WHAT HELPS ANOTHER BEST COMMUNICATE WITH YOU?

- To connect well, you need time to think and move around. Others should not fill in your words for you.
- To show caring, you like to receive hugs or pats on the back. You need time for silence to gather your own thoughts.
- To clear confusion, you want others to write or email or text you, then arrange a time to talk.
- If there is a significant disagreement, others should write you how they feel, and then give you time to respond. It's

best if you can call back while you are strolling or on a slow jog in nature.

- You are sensitive to tone of voice, so yelling will only shut you down. In text and emails, tone should be made explicit with language or emojis.
- To teach you a physical task, others should show you quickly and let you try it as soon as possible, asking questions as you go.

AVK—Auditorily Focuses, Visually Sorts, Kinesthetically Opens

Auditory, Visual, and Kinesthetic AVK PATTERN			
A1	👂	FOCUSED THINKING	To Trigger Concentration: AUDITORY
V2	👁	SORTING THINKING	To Trigger Sorting: VISUAL
K3	✋	OPEN THINKING	To Trigger Imagination: KINESTHETIC

> *We sing so much of love*
> *it's our largest industry our*
> *most marketable product*
> *and still we have not learned*
> *the songs of tenderness*
> *that might mend our*
> *broken hearts.*
>
> —NTOZAKE SHANGE

The AVK Snapshot

You can often out-talk most of the people around you, and are usually considered "smart" because you can easily verbalize thoughts and keep up with the pace of any conversation. Your words pour out in logical order, without hesitation, in a straightforward manner. You tend to speak in statements rather than questions. You tend to love facts, history, and ideas of all kinds. You are usually fascinated with language and can often learn to speak other tongues with ease. Music, the spoken word, humor, and puns are some of your delights.

You become focused and alert by bringing your attention to sounds and talking about the topic, then look around or write something. You generate insights by being in a silent place, then doodling or writing things out, and feeling the overall sensations in your body.

You rarely use hand gestures when you speak; when you do, it will be for emphasis only. Although you can maintain steady eye contact, your eyes will blink, twitch, or flutter if they try to sustain it too long. You often need to look away to find your words, usually to the side. You can see both the forest and the trees, visual details and the big picture.

You enjoy explaining, debating, discussing, and arguing almost any idea. You frequently use auditory vocabulary: "hear," "say," "sounds," "understand," or "That rings a bell," "Let's play it by ear," and "Talk to you soon." You are often shy about being touched and usually have a very sketchy sense of your body. You are capable of ignoring bodily signals for long periods of time. Many times, instead of expressing how you feel, you will articulately share the reasons for your feelings.

SKETCH: A MESSAGE FROM SOMEONE WHO USES THE AVK MIND PATTERN

I'd like to introduce myself because knowing a person's name and having him or her know mine is very important to me. The first thing you need to know is that I love spoken language and my life really centers around it. I am known for my verbal stamina—I can out-talk most of the people around me—and speaking in public is a breeze. I'm often told, though, that I don't speak about my emotions except in the abstract. I enjoy explaining, debating, discussing, and arguing almost any idea. I usually want to help others understand things from my point of view because I am able to describe the overall view of things.

I often get confused if people are hurt by what I say. For me, it's in one ear and out the other. I can easily remember people's names. I actually enjoy a good argument, as long as it doesn't get physical. I am quite proficient at entertaining people, and, if the truth be known, I do love to gossip. Sometimes I know I talk too much, but I enjoy making people laugh.

Memorizing verbal material is easy for me, and I also edit written material well because I can see the whole and details simultaneously. I'm aware that I haven't said much about the kinesthetic aspect of communication. Well, I shy away from casual touch of any kind; hugs feel far too personal and private. It's quite difficult for me to talk and feel at the same time. People have teased me about my lack of coordination, but I'd rather say that I'm creatively coordinated. Enough said!

AVK Characteristics

WHAT COMES NATURALLY?

- Explaining ideas verbally comes easily to you.
- Giving speeches and verbal reports or participating in heated discussions of all sorts is energizing.
- You see the big picture and the details at the same time.
- You can remember precisely what was said in previous conversations.
- You can comfortably sit still through long conversations.

WHAT HELPS YOU COMMUNICATE MOST EFFECTIVELY WITH ANOTHER?

- Recognize that others are not as facile with language as you are. Be aware you may have a tendency to interrupt

others and monopolize conversations. Refrain from finishing people's sentences. Allow for silent pauses as often
as possible so that others feel they have a chance to talk.

- To receive what others have to say, ask for a topic headline, such as "Are you saying you need a budget for our
vacation?"
- To communicate something that expresses feelings, consider doing it in writing first. It may be easier to express
feelings that way than to talk about them.
- Your communication style is to inspire others through understanding.

WHAT HELPS ANOTHER BEST COMMUNICATE WITH YOU?

- To connect well, you need verbal confirmations: "I hear
you!"
- To demonstrate caring, encourage others to tell you the
specific ways they care about you.
- To clear confusion, others should write down what they
hear you saying as well as what is important to them.
- If there is a significant disagreement, you want others to
tell you what they hear you saying, then write out what is
important to each of you and ask how you can both get
what you need.
- To teach you a physical task, others should be aware you
may struggle to do hands-on, technical skills. They should
give you verbal directions showing you step-by-step what
to do.

AKV — Auditorily Focuses, Kinesthetically Sorts, Visually Opens

Auditory, Kinesthetic, and Visual AKV PATTERN			
A1		FOCUSED THINKING	To Trigger Concentration: AUDITORY
K2		SORTING THINKING	To Trigger Sorting: KINESTHETIC
V3		OPEN THINKING	To Trigger Imagination: VISUAL

Better to be quarreling than lonesome.

—IRISH PROVERB

(and spoken like a true AKV)

The AKV Snapshot

You often have strong feelings and opinions, which you express easily. You are extremely articulate and have a high degree of physical energy right beneath the surface. You are a natural verbal leader, and love to take charge and tell everyone else what to do. You discuss, argue, or debate anything, tell jokes, and make plays on words. You can also be sarcastic. You tend to speak clearly, precisely, and with a lot of energy, feeling, and rhythm in your voice. More than anything, you want to inspire others with your words.

You best become focused when you are talking to others. You generate insights when you listen to quiet sounds or your own breathing while walking or gazing openly into space.

You remember what is said to you and often can repeat what you've heard word for word. This includes poetry, song lyrics, rhymes, and jokes. Hand gestures follow your words and punctuate what is being said.

Listening may not be easy for you. You may have the habit of interrupting others, especially if you are feeling a lot of excitement, unless you have been trained in debating or communication skills.

You tend to have an endless supply of physical energy that is not easily released. You are coordinated and can easily learn physical moves if given verbal instructions. You tend to be uncomfortable if confined to a desk or small space for any length of time.

You can be "eye-shy": Maintaining steady eye contact feels forced. You can be very particular about the visual images you choose—movies, television shows, and room decorations—since you are deeply influenced subconsciously by what you see. A nasty look from someone else can make a lasting impression on you.

SKETCH: A MESSAGE FROM SOMEONE WHO USES THE AKV MIND PATTERN

How's it going? I'm the kind of person who says what I feel and feels what I say. Let's just say I'm straightforward in how I communicate. I speak quickly and with a great deal of energy and feeling behind my words. I like telling it like it is. I love to laugh. I love to argue. I love to make other people laugh. I'm good at telling people what to do and how to do it. Coaching comes naturally. I've been told I bully people, but that's not true at all. I just like to motivate them. Sometimes people are way too sensitive to the tone of my voice. When I'm excited about something, I talk loud and energetically. I use sarcasm a lot, and I don't get why others don't just laugh it off. I love comedy and think laughter is the greatest medicine.

My feelings are right beneath the surface, and if I'm feeling something intensely, my mouth seems to have a mind of its own. As long as I maintain a daily physical practice of some kind and work out frequently at the gym, I stay balanced. Without that, I find myself overenergized. Physical activity seems to align disparate aspects of my life. Although it may be hard for you to know, I've always felt a great deal of sympathy for others in pain.

Writing is not easy for me. I like texts and Twitter. They relax me and seem to write themselves. When I read, it's just to scan, get an overview. I can process a lot of visual material quickly, but not actually read it in depth. I prefer to walk or at least stand or do something while we're talking. I've trained myself to look at people when I talk to them, but I am not comfortable doing it and my eyes get strained or twitch as a result. Even though I'd rather not look steadily at you, I love being seen and adored. Just kidding! Actually I do love being seen, just not examined too closely.

AKV Characteristics

WHAT COMES NATURALLY?

- You're a natural leader and coach; you love to tell others what to do.
- You see the big picture of something.
- You may be a great visionary thinker.
- You're comfortable giving speeches, verbal reports, or participating in discussions of all sorts.
- You can easily find the necessary words to teach someone else what to do.

WHAT HELPS YOU COMMUNICATE MOST EFFECTIVELY WITH ANOTHER?

- You need to recognize that other people may not be as facile at speaking as you are.
- You may have trouble listening and interrupt others, especially if you are feeling a lot of excitement. Even if you feel impatient when other people speak more slowly or less to the point than you want, don't finish other people's sentences.
- Check in with others as you talk. For example, "Are you with me?" or "Do you have any thoughts on this?"
- Be aware that people of other mind patterns, who may take you literally, can misunderstand sarcasm.

- To listen more comfortably, consider getting up and moving around or going for a walk with the other person.

WHAT HELPS ANOTHER BEST COMMUNICATE WITH YOU?

- To connect well, you want verbal confirmations: "I hear what you are saying."
- To show you caring, others should speak to you often, and you especially enjoy talking while "doing" something together: fishing, cooking.
- To clear confusion, you need a verbal headline, then to talk it out.
- If there is a significant disagreement, you need to walk or drive while you talk.
- If visuals are needed, keep it to one or two simple diagrams. You prefer a low amount of visual input, and dislike detailed writing or instructions.

We make assumptions all the time about when people are "paying attention" and when they're not. Now you know there is far more to it: where attention is directed, how it shifts, how it's triggered, and the natural differences for various mind patterns. Unless someone thinks exactly in the same way you do, it's oh-so-easy to misinterpret them altogether.

Your new understanding of mind patterns and how they relate to communication is a relational game changer. It's going to open possibilities for reconciling differences in ways that have never been apparent to you before.

In the next chapter we will explore three stories that illustrate using this discovery to navigate the uncharted terrain of another.

CHAPTER 3

Reconciling the Differences
in the Ways We Communicate

*The map may not be the territory but it sure helps you
to get around.*

—Peter A. Levine

We often refer to mind patterns as the hardware of thinking. The differences in our hardware often contribute to relational breakdowns, but they also hold the potential for breakthroughs. As we said previously, differences do not make someone else difficult. It's how we relate to those differences that makes or breaks a genuine connection. Discovering another person's mind pattern is like having an operator's manual for navigating differences.

We began this book explaining how different the two of us are. We shared with you how we had to learn to grow the relational intelligence between us. But the learning curve was steep: We stumbled, fell, pushed, crashed, and lurched our way over each other's attentional differences. Without awareness of mind patterns, the "we" would have quickly sunk as the two of us tried to collaborate as coauthors and business partners. By discovering and mapping how each of us communicates, we had a raft to travel the river of our differences and could move forward together. We kept afloat by centering and asking three questions each time we got stuck:

- How (not what) is each of us communicating?
- How is our communication affecting each other?
- How can I change the way I am communicating to have the effect I want?

This is the map of how our different mind patterns work when we are relating to each other.

ANGIE

Kinesthetic, Visual, and Auditory KVA PATTERN			
K1		FOCUSED THINKING	To Trigger Concentration: KINESTHETIC
V2		SORTING THINKING	To Trigger Sorting: VISUAL
A3		OPEN THINKING	To Trigger Imagination: AUDITORY

DAWNA

Visual, Auditory, and Kinesthetic VAK PATTERN			
V1		FOCUSED THINKING	To Trigger Concentration: VISUAL
A2		SORTING THINKING	To Trigger Sorting: AUDITORY
K3		OPEN THINKING	To Trigger Imagination: KINESTHETIC

We are ever mindful of the fact that Angie's mind uses the KVA mind pattern and Dawna's uses the VAK pattern. Because kinesthetic is the first attribute for Angie, movement helps her focus her attention. Given that Dawna uses the VAK pattern, movement opens her mind creatively. It also spaces her out. Even the search for a metaphor we could use to illustrate reconciling highlights our differences:

> ANGIE: How about if we call it a rope swing? (kinesthetic)
> DAWNA: Umm, what about a rainbow? (visual)
> ANGIE: We could say it's walking across a bridge?
> DAWNA: Let's say, "the way red and blue make purple."

If we didn't know how to work with these differences, we could make very negative misassumptions about each other. For instance, Angie could seem frenzied to Dawna because she moves around all the time. When Dawna has several documents open on her computer at the same time and is rapidly looking back and forth between them, Angie could think she's frenzied. Until we discovered our different mind patterns we could not really relate to *how* each other was thinking. Some of the rapids we had to learn to navigate are:

Dawna's mind organizes information visually. She needs several documents open at the same time. Angie's mind sorts visually and finds all the open documents chaotic. She organizes by moving paper around into piles. This triggers Dawna's mind into an open state and she spaces out when she wants to find something. Because she sorts information auditorily, she wants to talk out the confusion, but that just triggers Angie into a wide-open state of attention, making it difficult for her to find her own opinion.

Had we not recognized our communication differences for what they are, we would have fallen into the trap of attributing them to personality: "Angie's a fidgety scatterbrain who can't speak to her ideas." "Dawna talks too much and keeps going off track chaotically." When you recognize another's mind pattern, you can read their differences in a much more productive and positive way.

When she sees Angie pacing around the room, Dawna now knows that she is using kinesthetic input to become more focused on what we are doing. When she looks around the room it's now understood that she's sorting out thoughts. Angie now knows that when she sees Dawna studying one relevant document, she's focusing her attention. And that when Dawna wants to *discuss* something, she needs to sort through an issue.

In order to work remotely, we learned to use Skype to connect using as many senses as possible. When we are together, we use three computers, a treadmill, a Hula-Hoop, a mini trampoline, a whiteboard, piles of books, Post-its, and various Pandora radio stations to take each of us in and out of focused, sorting, and open attention. Discovering how to relate in an ongoing respectful way is as complex, surprising, and satisfying as creating a work of art.

Common Relational Breakdowns Due to Mind Pattern Misunderstandings

Here are some common relational tensions that result from not understanding differences in mind patterns:

AUDITORY

One's raised voice shuts the other down.
One talks all the time and the other can't get a word in edgewise.
One person shuts down verbally and the other interprets this as "the silent treatment."
One interrupts and fills in words for the other.

Visual

One looks away when the other is talking. This is inter-
preted as not paying attention.

One doesn't "show" they care—with gifts, eye contact,
dressing attractively, notes, or texts.

One makes frequent and long eye contact, and the other
feels invaded.

Kinesthetic

One is uncomfortable talking about feelings/emotions and
the other feels shut out and disconnected as a result because that's how they connect.

One of you is constantly on the go, needing to do things,
while the other likes to relax by being still, reading, or
listening to music.

One of you always initiates physical contact, the other
rarely or never does.

One hates to be interrupted or distracted while cooking or
doing something.

Mapping Another Person's Mind Pattern

Bring to mind someone with whom you'd like improved communication. Use the following as a checklist to help you find clues to
their mind pattern. Come back as often as needed to aid in your
discovery process. Remember, it is an adventure and sign of respect to want to know how someone else's mind processes information.

MIND PATTERN CHECKLIST

KINESTHETIC (HANDS-ON) FOCUSED (K1)
Prefers to do things with people rather than talk
Likes to make physical contact—handshake, pat on back, sit close
Well coordinated in his/her body
Uses kinesthetic language: "Let's do it," "Hard to grasp," "Get a handle"
Prefers to be in motion, standing, jiggling, playing with an object
Recalls action and physical environments easily
Organizes by piles
AUDITORY FOCUSED (A1)
Speaks confidently and has extensive vocabulary
Likes precision in language
Great verbal recall, little note-taking
Connects first with words
Uses auditory phrases: "Talk to you later," "Let's hear the points!"
VISUALLY FOCUSED (V1)
Steady eye contact
Likes visual order, lists, and color coding; visual precision
Lots of note-taking
Color coordinated and well dressed
Uses the phrases: "See you later," "Looks good," "Show me"
Gives visual descriptions of experiences
KINESTHETIC SORTING (K2)
Movement helps process emotions and sort possible action steps. Can be fidgety
May need to experience options and notice how they feel in order to choose. Often feels confused by different emotions simultaneously
Influenced emotionally and energetically by what they see and hear. May have difficulty distinguishing own feelings from others'
AUDITORY SORTING (A2)
Talking out loud helps get clear on personal thinking, opinions, beliefs
May talk a lot
May sound confusing to others when beginning to respond, get clearer as they talk it out
Often feels confused by too much conflicting inner self-talk

Likes wordplay, uses verbal metaphors to express themselves
Can understand and agree with both sides of a story, argument, and situation. Can talk and listen simultaneously, prefers overlapping conversations, interruptions are okay
Speaking has "ums" and "uhs," reflecting confusion, making space for shifts in thinking
Verbal clarity may come and go, depending on whether they are talking about what they see or what they feel/do
VISUAL SORTING (V2)
Writing about, diagramming, or seeing options helps them clarify choices
Can hold the overview and details simultaneously when writing, mapping, and editing. Can make 3-D images with eyes open and manipulate image to view from all angles
Often experiments with personal image in clothes, interests, handwriting
Can use images to express double meanings and to hold concepts
KINESTHETIC OPEN (K3)
Can sit easily for long periods of time
Shy about touch
Rarely talks about action
Physically still
Can be awkward physically
Private about feelings
AUDITORY OPEN (A3)
May take longer to speak, pauses between thoughts
Prefers to listen, then asks questions to engage everyone
May talk in circles or use creative words
Easily distracted by extraneous noises
Can space out listening to long verbal explanations
VISUALLY OPEN (V3)
Looks away frequently, can be eye-shy
Little or no note-taking. May not respond to emails, or responds with just a few words
Dresses for comfort rather than appearance
Prefers talking or doing to writing
Can space out if looking at lots of visual details or long emails

Notice where you have checked the most items for each state of attention—focused (A1, K1, or V1), sorting (A2, V2, K2), and open (A3, K3, V3). This will help you to discover which one of the six mind patterns most resembles the person about whom you are curious. If you need an overview of all the pattern combinations so you can compare, please see the appendix.

Reconciling Mind Pattern Differences

Once you have a guess about what the other person's mind pattern might be, you can increase your capacity to communicate with them by asking yourself three questions:

- How is each of us communicating?
- How is our communication affecting each other?
- How can I change the way I am communicating to have the effect I want?

The following is a guide for reconciling some of the most common relational differences due to mind patterns. It will help you remember to shift your attention so you can communicate more effectively. The first column describes a difference that's commonly misinterpreted and a breakdown that you may be encountering as a result. The second column indicates how that difference can be understood through mind patterns. The third column offers suggestions on how to reconcile with this difference based on the experiences of various people we have worked with.

A GUIDE FOR RECONCILING MIND PATTERN DIFFERENCES

COMMUNICATION DIFFERENCE	RECOGNIZING COMMUNICATION DIFFERENCES	SUGGESTIONS FOR RECONCILIATION
I shut down and lose interest in the conversation when others talk too much or talk over me.	Auditory triggers open attention for me, and I get overwhelmed by too much verbal communication. I recognize that for others this may be different; auditory may help them focus.	• I give myself permission to get up and walk around. • I ask others to slow their verbal tempo down a little, and pause to give me time to ask questions so I can stay engaged. • I bring an art journal to meetings, coffee dates, and appointments so I can doodle while we are in discussion.
I miss important details in emails and notes, and get overwhelmed by texts. Often I forget to respond or if I do it's with one or two words. Others think that I am curt.	Visual triggers open attention for me, and I get agitated with long emails or too many details in text. I recognize that for most people it's an easy, convenient form of communication.	• I request that colleagues and friends make the subject line an explicit action such as "Please respond by 3 P.M." I can then follow up with a call. • I share that I prefer they keep emails as short as possible. • I ask that we use Skype or FaceTime for calls.
I don't easily recall the specifics of what we've talked about in our recent conversations.	Auditory triggers open attention for me. I recognize that for others recalling specific details from the conversation is important.	• I now type notes into my smartphone, particularly when my partner and I are working with a therapist or confirming plans for the kids. • I ask my wife to send me a friendly note following a talk, recapping the conversation. • I posted a photo of my mom and myself above my desk with a note: "Loved our talk about love, and what makes a great marriage." I look at the picture and remember the whole conversation.

COMMUNICATION DIFFERENCE	RECOGNIZING COMMUNICATION DIFFERENCES	SUGGESTIONS FOR RECONCILIATION
I tend to talk in circles, and others just want me to get to the point.	Auditory triggers sorting attention for me. While it's helpful for me, I recognize that others may be frustrated as they try to follow my train of thought.	• I request that others ask me questions to help clarify my thinking. • I find it helpful to have others repeat back to me: "So what you're saying is . . ." This helps me sift through thoughts to get to what I was trying to say.
I need to talk through both sides of a situation to make a decision and tend to vacillate.	Auditory triggers sorting attention. I recognize that for others this may sound wishy-washy.	• On paper I make two columns to write down the pros and cons. • Rather than talking it all out at once, I speak first to the cons, and then the pros. This makes the difference between them more discernible.
I appear jittery, and anxious to move. I am told that I fiddle a lot and it appears I am not listening.	Kinesthetic triggers focused attention for me. I recognize that others may think I am not interested in what they are saying.	• I walk around the room while I talk out ideas. • I schedule meetings over coffee at places with paper tablecloths where I can doodle while talking. • I do things like unload the dishwasher, clean, and garden while my partner and I talk. It helps me focus, since I love doing two things at once.

COMMUNICATION DIFFERENCE	RECOGNIZING COMMUNICATION DIFFERENCES	SUGGESTIONS FOR RECONCILIATION
I am intense with my words, and love a good discussion. To others I may seem overbearing, but I love to talk.	Auditory triggers focused attention for me. I recognize that others may think I talk too much.	• I created a signal for myself: In meetings every time I take a sip of water, I remember there are others in the discussion, too, and to pause and ask for their opinion. • I tell others up front in a joking way that I have a lot of energy when I talk, and to not feel rude if they need to interrupt me. • I joined Toastmasters and actually coach others in speaking. I love doing this.

RECONCILIATION IN ACTION

Depending on your mind pattern, some of you will absorb this rich content most effectively from charts, but others will absorb this material best by imagining it in context. Toward that end, let's eavesdrop on a client who described her communication difficulties to Angie.

"Sometimes it's as if I don't exist. Paul's impossible!" Julie complained. We were hiking the Wasatch Mountains in early spring. Unaware of the green buds peeking through the snow and mud, she trudged on furiously. "I've waited three years for this research project to get funded and finally it was approved. Last night there I was sitting on the leather couch, all excited because I could finally tell my beloved husband the project had been funded." Her neck muscles tightened as she continued. "He raced around the kitchen unpacking groceries. He wouldn't even look at me! I told him to stop for one damn minute but he kept moving around, ignoring me. I just lost it.

He's totally insensitive—he doesn't pay attention to me when I most need him to." She rolled her eyes and continued, "Then he rushed over to me and tried to give me a hug, but it was too late. I stormed out and didn't even tell him my news."

"Julie," I asked, "how do you know when a person is present and paying attention to you?" Without hesitation she told me that he would look her in the eye, and listen to what she had to say while sitting still. "Which is why Paul hurt me so much last night, when he blatantly ignored me," she said.

"Okay, before we get into Paul, I'd like to ask you to get present with me in this moment." She blinked, looked at me with a confused expression, and asked, "What do you mean?"

I replied, "You just shared with me that for *you*, paying attention means looking a person in the eye, and listening while totally still. So do that with me now." She came over and stood still across from me just as I asked. Her gaze softened as she looked at me and took in the sounds of the birds chirping. Her shoulders dropped and she breathed easily as she told me she was now present and listening.

"Okay, now back to Paul. What effect did you want the way you were communicating to have on him?"

"I wanted him to see my excitement, and know I had something important to say."

I wanted her to understand that his initial response could be due to their communication differences. "What happened when you didn't get this effect?" I asked.

"I got pissed, and didn't want to even speak to him. I didn't know what else to do."

I decided to use my hands to show her how the three states of attention worked, and clasped them in a tight ball. Then I asked her to imagine this as a focused state. "For you, seeing and being seen triggers you into this state."

I then opened my fingers and clasped them loosely so that there was space between the fingers. "Next, your mind naturally goes into a sorting state to tell the whole story. Which explains why it was so important for you to be listened to." She nodded slowly, intrigued.

I then unlaced my fingers and moved my hands until they were wide apart. "Next, your mind opens into a state of attention where you are the most sensitive. This is where your feelings of excitement and sadness are. It's why feeling Paul next to you instead of unpacking groceries would have been more satisfying, right?" I was describing the VAK pattern her mind used to communicate.

She nodded yes, tears sliding down her cheeks, then asked, "So why doesn't Paul just look at me, listen, and sit still if he really wants to connect with me?"

I held my two hands out in front. "These are hands, but the right is different from the left. Your mind and Paul's shift into these focused, sorting, and open states with different triggers."

Her eyes got wide as she realized the implications of their different mind patterns. "Moving may actually *help* him listen?" I nodded acknowledgment.

She then said, "You know, when we first got married, I used to sit on a stool in the garage while he did his woodwork. We had the best talks there. I shared stories, and he'd ask question after question. How did I forget that?"

She closed her eyes when I asked her to use her imagination to replay what happened last night, but this time incorporating the new understanding she had of their mind pattern differences. She opened her hazel eyes very wide, looked right at me, and said, "Now I get that when he was putting away the groceries, it was his way of giving me his focused attention while I talked. And that must be why when I turned away from his hug, he felt rejected." She tilted her head and asked me, "Am I getting it right?"

"Rather than you and me guessing, why don't you and Paul discover it together? Do some experiments. It's just doing relational research."

She lit up, and reached over, putting her arm around me. This was no casual thing considering what we learned about her mind pattern. "Maybe he's not really that impossible after all."

The graphic and descriptions below illustrate the mind pattern differences that Julie and Paul were trying to reconcile.

VAK⇔KAV

Visual, Auditory, and Kinesthetic VAK PATTERN				Kinesthetic, Auditory, and Visual KAV PATTERN			
V1	👁	FOCUSED THINKING	To Trigger Concentration: VISUAL	K1	✋	FOCUSED THINKING	To Trigger Concentration: KINESTHETIC
A2	👂	SORTING THINKING	To Trigger Sorting: AUDITORY	A2	👂	SORTING THINKING	To Trigger Sorting: AUDITORY
K3	✋	OPEN THINKING	To Trigger Imagination: KINESTHETIC	V3	👁	OPEN THINKING	To Trigger Imagination: VISUAL

Differences to Navigate

- Paul, who uses the KAV pattern, will be very prone to give hugs and engage in physical touch or activity. He may not understand why Julie, who uses the VAK pattern, is inclined to sit still for long periods.
- Julie wants visual tidiness, while Paul will organize in loose piles; this may cause some angst between them.
- Julie may not understand how important "feeling good" and physical comfort are to Paul when it comes to his space and their surroundings.
- Julie overwhelms Paul with visual details. She takes his direct eye contact or lack thereof personally.

Creating Conditions for Reconciling Differences Through Communication

- When Julie wants to share a vision that is important, it will help her be clear if she writes it down first, then talks about it to Paul, who will help her turn it into concrete action.

- When they find themselves arguing, it will be most effective for them to go for a walk to talk it out so that Paul can look wherever he wants, and Julie can stay in touch with her feelings. This will help each of them know what they really need and describe how they are feeling.
- To calm and center themselves, they could sit back-to-back and listen to calming music.
- It's most natural for Julie to express her love by writing and telling Paul how she feels. A short and romantic note affects him deeply. Likewise, when Julie is touched with care or receives a gift, she is more likely to see she is loved.
- It's most natural for Paul to express his love through actions and words.

As you read the above, who in your life comes to mind as someone with whom you want to communicate more effectively? It may be someone you're misunderstanding, or want to connect with more meaningfully. Use the previous chapter to find the closest fit for each of your mind patterns, then use the **guide for reconciling mind pattern differences on pages 60–62.**

In the appendix, you can also read more about every combination of mind patterns as well as further suggestions for communicating effectively.

Even emotional wounds that have festered between two people for decades can heal when they find a way to reconcile their communication differences. There are none more touchy or touching than those between a parent and child, as the following story of Dawna guiding a woman back to her grown son—and her own heart—illustrates.

Janice spoke just four words as she buckled herself into the passenger seat of my car. "I hate my son." Her voice was scraped out, hollow, as if she had been crying without tears. In the six months I had known her, I'd never experienced Janice, the CEO of a large organization, like this. We had previously discovered together that her mind used the VKA pattern. It organized visually: She dressed impeccably, maintained steady eye contact, and meticulously made one list after another. Janice liked to think things over and sort them out kinesthetically while she worked out in a gym or walked in nature. She had to use her hands when she spoke and her words often looped from one question to another, signs that auditory input triggered an open state of mind.

I had met her oldest son, William, when he was a struggling college student. From what I remembered, he spoke in sarcastic, assertive exclamation points. His mind didn't "do" questions. He dressed for comfort in loose-fitting clothes that didn't match and he moved easily and constantly, making large and swooping gestures that followed his words. He was, however, visually shy, barely looking at someone before glancing away. For all these reasons I assumed his mind used the AKV pattern. He described himself as a laid-back kind of guy. Except when he was around his mother . . . then he changed into Noxious Ninja Man. It was my assessment that their minds used exactly opposite patterns to think, what I call "unlived parentheses," meaning that what was most awake and active in him was most dormant and receptive in her. What focused his mind— auditory input—triggered her into a wide-open state of mind. And vice versa: What focused her mind—visual input— triggered him into a wide-open attentional state.

In spite of knowing their differences, I was stunned when I heard Janice say with such vehemence that she hated her son. The only thing I could do was breathe deeply and offer simple caring for the pain that had to be hiding under all that intensity. I knew she needed to come into the present moment with me first, so she could ground all of those feelings the way a shoreline receives breaking waves. I suggested we drive to the

Visual, Kinesthetic, and Auditory VKA PATTERN			Auditory, Kinesthetic, and Visual AKV PATTERN		
V1	FOCUSED THINKING	To Trigger Concentration: VISUAL	A1	FOCUSED THINKING	To Trigger Concentration: AUDITORY
K2	SORTING THINKING	To Trigger Sorting: KINESTHETIC	K2	SORTING THINKING	To Trigger Sorting: KINESTHETIC
A3	OPEN THINKING	To Trigger Imagination: AUDITORY	V3	OPEN THINKING	To Trigger Imagination: VISUAL

ocean and walk silently next to each other for a while. Step-by-step, I was thinking about the riddle of a mother and a son caught in a riptide created by their different ways of thinking, knowing, and communicating.

Ten minutes of looking at the ocean and walking in silence reversed the tide for Janice. I took a small mirror out of my pocket, passed it to her, and said, "Look into this and ask yourself what effect you want to have on your son." I thought that seeing her own face and hearing her own words would make it possible for her to know what she was really feeling.

Janice looked briefly into the mirror and then shook her head before telling me that William yelled terrible things at her and left a mess in the kitchen just to piss her off because he knew she couldn't stand looking at it. In addition, she described how he dressed like a slob, and refused to look at her. This proved, she insisted, that he really disrespected her, and would never love her. This may seem illogical but the heart has its own logic, as you probably know very well.

Wanting to bring her back to the present, I decided to refocus her attention visually and kinesthetically by asking her to tell me out loud what she was seeing around her and the sensations she was feeling in her body as we continued to walk along the water's edge. After a few minutes, her breath dropped down into her belly and the muscles around her jaw softened. I felt her with me, finally, so I repeated my question gently, "I have heard the effect he's had on you, but what effect do *you* really want to have on him?"

Janice's jaw muscles tightened again and her lips stretched, tight and thin. Out of the corner of her mouth, she said, "He doesn't care. He wouldn't listen anyway. If he respected me, he would know how to treat his own mother."

Years of being a professional thinking partner has taught me that a person often wants *from* someone else what they most need to give *to* them. I mentioned this and asked if the effect she wanted to have on him was that he know she cared and had done her best to treat him well. She rolled her mossy green eyes and said nothing. I let the quiet be for a while. Since her "hate" had now become "disrespect," it seemed we had made some progress.

I suspected having opposite mind patterns was playing a large part in what seemed like irreconcilable differences: Her son was assertive in the ways her mind was most sensitive, and vice versa.

She began to walk faster and faster and then stopped abruptly. Turning to face me, she threw her hands in the air and asked, "How in the world could he not know that I care? I buy him fabulous clothes which he never wears. I send him cards and little notes. I invite him to events and movies . . ."

Knowing that she organized her world visually, I was curious what would happen to her intense, chaotic feelings if she could see that she was needed by him. I suggested we go into a charming little restaurant I knew up ahead. As we sat sipping wine at a corner table, I made a suggestion. "Let's assume that you are giving him what *you* most need, but that he doesn't really know how to communicate to you that he respects and cares for you. Tell me again how you would know if he did."

I moved next to her and as Janice ticked off each behavior, I wrote it down on the paper tablecloth. When the whole list was sprawled out there in front of us, I scribbled the following words on the top of the "page": "To show me you care about me . . ." There were more than thirty things on the list including: 1) Ask me questions about my life. 2) Tell me you love me. 3) Dress so you look neat. 4) Look at me when I talk to you. 5) Clean up the kitchen after you use it. 6) Hug me like you mean it when you leave instead of slamming the door.

I finally asked her the one question that would not leave my mind: "Have you ever told William all of this?" She shook her head, then looked sheepishly down at her hands.

I knew that if William had written a list to Janice, it would be very different. In fact, it wouldn't even be natural for him to write it. He'd just blurt it out verbally as if he was a coach shouting plays to his team. Those differences were what made relating to each other so challenging. But if they could learn how to change the ways they were communicating to each other, there was great possibility they would reconcile. In a certain way, the list we had created together on the tablecloth was an operator's manual to her heart.

By the time we were back in my office, I realized Janice needed to see, feel, and hear what had been buried under the submerged tentacles of hatred. I read the list back to her, very slowly. Tears slid down her cheeks. I suggested she write the list in her own hand as a letter to William. At first she hesitated, saying that he was lazy and would never read it. I reassured Janice that she didn't necessarily have to show it to him; what was important was that *she* get to see it on the outside instead of feeling it tangled inside her heart.

She grabbed my best pen and wrote without pause while I finished a whole glass of sparkling water, and then another. Finally, her hand floated above the paper and she paused for just a moment before leaning over and adding two last words. Then Janice released a long breath and sank back into the brown leather couch.

I took the letter and read it slowly out loud. As I spoke those two last words, she wrapped her arms around herself and swayed gently back and forth as if what she had heard were a mooring post to which she had tied her heart. They were: "Love, Mom."

It was more than a month before I heard from Janice again. To my surprise, she had scheduled a Skype video call for the three of us. She told me they wanted to share what they had been learning together after Janice had given William the letter. True to his AKV mind pattern, William began speaking immediately, emphatically. What surprised me was that Janice put her hands over her ears. He took the signal and immediately stood up, walked around, and asked his mother a question. He continued to pace for the remainder of the call, glancing over at her occasionally to show he was with her, but not overloading his visually sensitive mind by trying to sustain eye contact. I was ecstatic that they had figured out a way to accommodate each of their mind patterns, no longer helpless victims to each other's differences.

A year later, Janice was diagnosed with terminal brain cancer, and died soon after. William was at her side daily, whispering encouragement, telling her secret jokes, stroking her hand tenderly. They had learned to connect with love and respect just in time.

The story of Janice and William highlights the challenges that can occur when opposite mind patterns collide. But it also points to something that is true for everyone: As you learned in chapter 1, when the light of your attention is highly focused, your open attention, like the deepest and widest ocean floor, can disappear into the shadows. Without realizing it, you leave your inner world "unattended" and your awareness of what you really feel and need disappears. Janice was so focused on what was wrong with William that she didn't know what she needed or how to communicate it effectively.

The opposite can also be true. When you are completely internally focused, your ability to register what may be going on for another person and the effect you are having on them is diminished. Very few of us have ever been taught how to be connected to another person without losing awareness of our inner self. How you relate to others is strengthened through awareness of your ebbs and flows of different states of attention.

Bring to mind the Möbius strip you made in chapter 1. The turning point in that strip is a place where you have great influence because it is where you can shift your inner and outer awareness. It is a place to pause between impulse and action to find out what each of you needs in the moment. Janice was at this turning point when she became fully present walking on the beach, looked in the mirror, and considered the effect *she* was having on her son. That created an opening to reconcile their differences.

Did a particular person or relationship come to mind as you read about Janice and William? When you allow yourself to get curious at the turning point of the Möbius strip, what differences do you discover that you need to navigate? What internal needs of yours are going unexpressed and unmet, for example, to be heard, seen, touched, verbally appreciated, etc.? What questions can you ask to discover the unexpressed needs of the other person? Use the descriptions of the different mind pattern pairings in the appendix to help you.

Remember the trim-tab? You've been exploring how to discover and reconcile communication differences in one small but not insignificant way. At first this might feel awkward because it requires your mind to let go of the comfortable and habitual ways you relate to significant others. But then, your first kiss was awkward, too, wasn't it? Curiosity is a natural state, though it may seem to be no big thing. We encourage you to follow its current; let it open your mind and it will guide the growth of the intelligence that connects you to those who are most important to you.

In the next section you'll learn how to navigate differences in how each of you thinks in order to bring you more alive.

Discovery Two:

UNDERSTAND

Different Ways of Understanding—
Through the Discovery of Thinking Talents

CHAPTER 4

Mapping the Way
You Understand

*Days pass and the years vanish, and we walk, unknow-
ing, amongst miracles.*

—Sabbath prayer

When we work with someone to reconcile differences the word we
hear most often is "understand": "She just doesn't understand
me." "If only he could understand." "I just don't understand her."
"I don't understand how he and I could ever . . ." But when we
ask, "How would you know if they *did* understand you?" the person usually stares blankly into space, shrugs, and says, "I'd just
know." In our collective eight decades or so of clinical and personal training about communication and psychology, we have
heard professors use the word "understanding" many times, but
none has defined it or described how this essential element of
human connection is created within and between people.

Our research and professional experience has led us to recognize that each person needs very different kinds of thinking to
"understand." We call these particular ways of understanding
thinking talents. They are indigenous to you, natural preferences

that energize you. If mind patterns are like different musical instruments, thinking talents are like different styles of music: jazz, baroque, or hip-hop. Discovering your mind patterns helps you know how to play your instrument to communicate well. Thinking talents help you know what style of music you want to play on that instrument. Both mind patterns and thinking talents refer to *how* you are thinking, not *what* you are thinking. Discovering what *you need* is the domain of this chapter. Discovering how to recognize and reconcile the differences in understanding between *you and another* is explored in the next chapter.

Before we share our working definition of understanding, we'd like to ask you to make it relevant to your own life through a little thought experiment: Bring to mind a time when you knew someone really understood you. Step into the memory as if it were happening now. How does that person communicate understanding to you? What do you feel, see, and hear?

Now turn your mind to a time when you really understood someone else and they knew it. Specifically, what were the elements that helped you understand them and how did you communicate it?

Our definition of understanding is coherence within you as well as between you and another. All the individual elements of the best of your thinking—such as analysis, empathy, connection with others, idea generation—are working with one another harmoniously to create a resonance.

Understanding softens your heart and strengthens your intellect. It insists that you evolve. It allows you to chip away at your own bewilderment until you find a pattern, which enables you to withstand the challenges and losses in your life and grow from them.

The word "understanding" is derived from the ancient Greek word *epistamai,* which translates as "I know how I know." This chapter explores exactly that: how each person has a different way of knowing how he or she knows.

Misunderstanding: What's Missing from Understanding?

In our society more and more people are feeling alienated, disenfranchised, and marginalized. There's a desperate need to feel understood. What is frequently offered in its place is a quick fix, patronizing advice, indifference, or medication. Marci, a woman Dawna worked with recently, put it this way: "I don't feel that many men have ever listened to me, not my father, my boss, my husband, my son, or even my therapist. What I want from all of them is a little understanding. Is that too much to ask? When I said all of this to my therapist, he told me he was proud of me for being so assertive. I almost choked him. He hadn't understood a word I said."

Lest you attribute this to a gender issue, Steve, a man who was a client of Angie's, put it this way: "When I begin to share with my girlfriend what's really on my mind, what she gives me is advice. The same goes for my sister, who offers me a wide assortment of seemingly easy solutions. I want them to understand what I'm experiencing. I want someone to finally understand what I want and need."

Few people know what they need in order to understand or what's missing in order for them to feel understood. Explore your own experience: Think about a time when you felt really misunderstood by someone. As you step into that memory, notice what was missing. What did you or didn't you see, hear, and feel that would have made all the difference to you? Now think of a time when you really misunderstood someone else. What was missing for you?

In our experience, five things are missing from our understanding of one another and ourselves. Let's explore them in detail.

What's Missing Is Curiosity

What we are really asking of you in these little thought experiments is to bring curiosity to your own experience as you would to a riddle. When you think of the most understanding people you have ever known, chances are they share one defining trait: curiosity. Motivated by a desire to explore the unfamiliar, they are drawn toward what they don't understand. They can hold the awkwardness of not knowing with curiosity long enough to recognize their own and another's needs. They discover what is familiar in a whole new way, a way that grows the boundaries of what they thought possible.

When we work with people who believe their differences are irreconcilable, there is no curiosity to be found. It is as if their belief has become a wall between them that makes understanding impossible. Sometimes the wall is blank. They just don't know why they don't feel understood, or understand the other person. Sometimes it's too tall to see or climb over. Sometimes it's covered with blood from all the times both people have banged their heads against it, shrugged, and turned their backs to it.

Some of the walls we have encountered are covered with the graffiti of exasperation drawn in black or scarlet: "You're an imbecile!" "I can't stand you." "No entry." "No exit." "No U-turns." As an alternative, we encourage one or both people to rest their foreheads gently against the wall or rest their aching backs on its solidity and stare at the clouds in the sky, as they did when they were children, seeking curiosity, wondering what each of them really needs.

If this much is possible, we know we're on our way to understanding. Because at some point, curiosity will enable at least one of them to get on their knees and begin to dig, to dig down into the rich, dark dirt of not knowing what to do, what to say, where to go, or what to think. We encourage them to dig a tunnel through the rocks and rigidities of their habits of thinking, and eventually turn that tunnel toward the other person to discover what really matters. This is where understanding begins. This is where reconciliation begins.

What's Missing Is the Best of Your Thinking

What makes this digging so difficult is that people are far more familiar with the worst of their thinking than the best. There is an old Hasidic tale about wise men who wore jackets with two pockets and women who wore aprons with two pockets. Both the men and the women put a handful of dirt in one pocket and a few gold coins in the other, to remind themselves of both their ordinary humanity and the gifts they bring to the rest of the world. We think of the dirt as the thinking habits you use to build the wall between you and someone who understands differently. Since you were very small, you have been reminded of your deficits, your mistakes, your failures, your limitations, and your pathologies. From the first spelling test, the first time you reached to Mommy and poked her eye with an oatmeal-covered finger, your attention was directed to what was wrong. Your attention was directed to the dirt in the pocket.

Think of the gold coins as the best of your thinking. You were never given a way of identifying it or understanding its value. You may even have been warned that talking about the gold coins— your inner assets, your abilities, your talents—would cause you to have a swelled head, an inflated ego. You were asked, "Who do you think you are?"

Prepare yourself to pump up just a little, because the digging needed to get under that wall is a kind of treasure hunt for those gold coins, for the ways of thinking that naturally energize you when you use them and help you understand. You may have athletic talents or creative talents, but your thinking talents are aspects of your cognitive capacity. They aren't skills because you don't learn them per se. And they aren't personality traits because they are aspects of how you think, not how you feel. They appear to be inborn, part of your cognitive capacity, in the same way that a particular understanding of rhythm comes to some people and the talent of perfect pitch comes to others. At this particular moment, you may not believe you have any or may not know what they are. All we ask of you is encapsulated in these two words said by sages for centuries: Be curious.

What's Missing Is Knowing How to Discover Your Thinking Talents

In the last twenty-five years, it has been discovered that the brain uses more energy than any other organ in the human body. This explains why so many people talk about being "burned out." Are there ways of thinking that can generate energy, rather than drain it? Have you ever experienced being "in the zone" while focusing on something and time completely disappeared? No matter how long you were at it, you still felt fully energized. Chances are very high that you were using one or more of your thinking talents.

At a series of retreats we led in 2005 for senior business leaders who were searching for a new direction in their career, we conducted many brief videotaped interviews. We asked people a wide variety of questions about their approaches to work, friendships, and challenges. In reviewing them with the whole group we noticed that it was possible to actually see someone "light up" and become more alive when they were thinking about a problem *in a particular way*. It became obvious to all of us that there were certain times that the faces of those interviewed would literally shine. What was energizing each person's thinking? We were completely fascinated and determined to know more.

When working as thinking partners to CEOs and senior leadership teams, we continued to search for tools and processes that gave clues to what energized specific ways of thinking for particular people. We came across the work of Donald O. Clifton of the Gallup organization, who developed interviews that allowed businesses to identify talents in individuals in order to match people to the right roles. He partnered with Marcus Buckingham to write the book *Now, Discover Your Strengths*, which promoted the idea that a person would produce the best results by making the most of what they called "signature strengths" instead of overemphasizing weaknesses or perceived deficiencies. They identified thirty-four ways of thinking that people habitually use to approach challenges.

Over time, we have integrated what we learned from Gallup into our own work, sharing it with each of our thinking partners and with global teams. Leaders from The Hague to Houston were fascinated by understanding how differences in thinking could help them connect, rather than divide by the diversity issues of culture and gender. The work grew and changed based on our experience and as that happened, we came up with this idea of thinking talents rather than signature strengths. We felt this terminology acknowledged and emphasized that each person has talents of thinking, as well as of sports, music, or art. Identifying them in this way has led the leaders to value the contributions they could make as well as being more open to one another's expertise. They have increased their collaborative thinking in domains where they previously had misunderstandings. Since their thinking talents generated energy, boring team meetings began to light up with aliveness, which was a veritable miracle in and of itself. We have continued to explore how this is also true in family systems, nonprofits, and small businesses. In each setting, identifying thinking talents helps people begin to understand how they can connect to one another, lean on one another, and live *with* one another in a more vitally and naturally interdependent way.

Since it's very difficult to see, hear, or feel when you light up and then analyze what thinking talents you were using in that situation, we developed the following self-assessment to help you discover the best of your cognitive capacity. When Marci, the woman who felt so misunderstood by the men in her life, completed the assessment, she discovered that her thinking talents were all highly relational: Feeling for Others, Adapting, Connection, Creating Intimacy, Believing. This helped her know exactly what to ask for when she needed to feel understood. It also helped her recognize what she needed to give to herself when she felt lost. Steve, Angie's client, discovered that his talents were Storytelling, Collecting, Humor, Making Order, and Precision. When he experienced others thinking with him in those ways, he felt completely understood.

Now it's your turn to discover what lights you up and energizes your brain. This assessment works like a card game. As you read the thirty-five "cards" that follow, sort them into three categories. The first category is for cards that describe: **"This ALWAYS gives me energy."** The second is for cards that describe: **"This SOMETIMES gives me energy."** The third is for cards that describe: **"This NEVER gives me energy."** To help you with this, you will see that each thinking talent card has a label at the bottom that reads "Always-Sometimes-Never." We suggest you take a piece of paper and create three columns with these labels. As you go through the cards, write the talents in the appropriate columns.

For something to rank in the "This ALWAYS gives me energy" pile, you should be able to say the following about it:

- This is one of your innate ways of thinking. That is, you've always been really good at doing this, even if you never had any specific training, and you always prefer to use this descriptor when approaching challenges.
- You get natural joy and energy from using this thinking talent, and it doesn't burn you out.
- You excel in using this talent and enjoy developing your capacity with it.

Understanding these aspects will help you distinguish thinking talents from skills, personality traits, or other capacities.

Once you have placed all of the talents into one of the three categories, go to the "**ALWAYS**" group and edit it down to *five to eight* of your strongest talents. If you have more than eight, ask yourself which ones have always been true for you, and always will be true for you; eliminate those that aren't quite as strong. If you have fewer than five, go to the "**SOMETIMES**" group and transfer the strongest ones there to the "**ALWAYS**" group until you have at least five in "**ALWAYS**." You may find that one or more talents in your "**ALWAYS**" group seem irrelevant to you, but if they fit the above criteria, please consider them thinking talents anyway. The five to eight cards remaining in the "**ALWAYS**" group will most accurately describe what you consider to be your dominant thinking talents.

There is no way you can be wrong about your self-assessment. As your awareness of thinking talents increases, you may notice things about yourself you had not before, and may need to reconsider some of your choices. As your understanding grows, you can always change your mind.

©PTP 2016

THINKING TALENTS

Adapting

"How can I adapt to what's happening now?"

Lives in the moment and discovers the future one choice at a time; expects and enjoys detours. Flexible, easily adjusts to change.

Always -Sometimes -Never

THINKING TALENTS

Believing

"Does this mesh with my beliefs?"

High ethics as guide to behavior; people know where they stand. Makes decisions based on their values.

Always -Sometimes -Never

THINKING TALENTS

Creating Intimacy

"How can I be closer and more genuine with the people I already know?"

Comfortable with intimacy; encourages deepening of relationships; "the more that is shared together, the more that is risked together." May have a challenge meeting new people.

Always -Sometimes -Never

THINKING TALENTS

Collecting

"What am I interested in here?"

Collects information, things, quotations, artifacts or facts, anything that is deemed interesting. The world is exciting because of its variety; acquiring, compiling, and filing stuff away keeps things fresh.

Always -Sometimes -Never

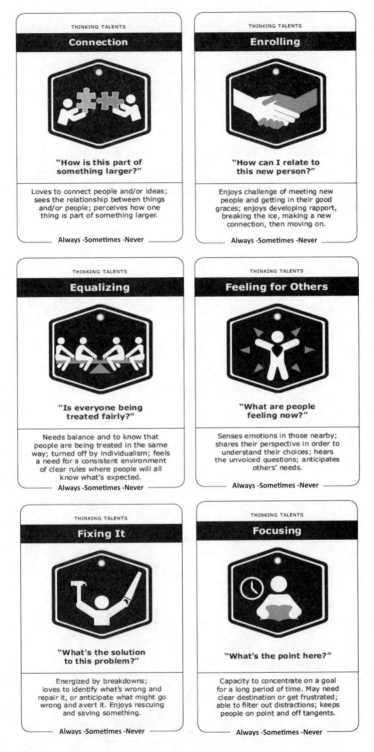

THINKING TALENTS

Connection

"How is this part of something larger?"

Loves to connect people and/or ideas; sees the relationship between things and/or people; perceives how one thing is part of something larger.

Always -Sometimes -Never

THINKING TALENTS

Enrolling

"How can I relate to this new person?"

Enjoys challenge of meeting new people and getting in their good graces; enjoys developing rapport, breaking the ice, making a new connection, then moving on.

Always -Sometimes -Never

THINKING TALENTS

Equalizing

"Is everyone being treated fairly?"

Needs balance and to know that people are being treated in the same way; turned off by individualism; feels a need for a consistent environment of clear rules where people will all know what's expected.

Always -Sometimes -Never

THINKING TALENTS

Feeling for Others

"What are people feeling now?"

Senses emotions in those nearby; shares their perspective in order to understand their choices; hears the unvoiced questions; anticipates others' needs.

Always -Sometimes -Never

THINKING TALENTS

Fixing It

"What's the solution to this problem?"

Energized by breakdowns; loves to identify what's wrong and repair it, or anticipate what might go wrong and avert it. Enjoys rescuing and saving something.

Always -Sometimes -Never

THINKING TALENTS

Focusing

"What's the point here?"

Capacity to concentrate on a goal for a long period of time. May need clear destination or get frustrated; able to filter out distractions; keeps people on point and off tangents.

Always -Sometimes -Never

THINKING TALENTS
Get to Action

"What can I do right now?"

Impatient for action rather than contemplation. Must make something happen.

Always -Sometimes -Never

THINKING TALENTS
Goal Setting

"What can I accomplish today?"

The daily drive to accomplish something and meet a goal. Every day starts at 0 and must achieve something tangible. There is a perpetual whisper of discontent.

Always -Sometimes -Never

THINKING TALENTS
Having Confidence

"What, me worry?"

Knows he or she is able to deliver. Self-assured; no one can tell him or her what to think. They alone have the authority to reach their own conclusions.

Always -Sometimes -Never

THINKING TALENTS
Humor

"What is amusing about this?"

Enjoys finding the humor in situations. Can lighten tense moments and puts self and others at ease with laughter.

Always -Sometimes -Never

THINKING TALENTS
Including

"How can I stretch the circle wider?"

Desires to make others feel a part of the group so as many as possible can feel its support; no one should be on the outside looking in; accepting, nonjudgmental.

Always -Sometimes -Never

THINKING TALENTS
Innovation

"How can this be done differently?"

Loves to create new processes or products; easily bored with routine. Energized by never having done it before.

Always -Sometimes -Never

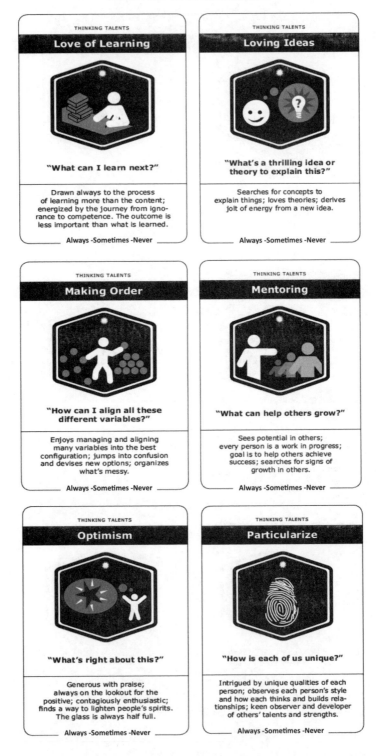

THINKING TALENTS

Love of Learning

"What can I learn next?"

Drawn always to the process of learning more than the content; energized by the journey from ignorance to competence. The outcome is less important than what is learned.

Always -Sometimes -Never

THINKING TALENTS

Loving Ideas

"What's a thrilling idea or theory to explain this?"

Searches for concepts to explain things; loves theories; derives jolt of energy from a new idea.

Always -Sometimes -Never

THINKING TALENTS

Making Order

"How can I align all these different variables?"

Enjoys managing and aligning many variables into the best configuration; jumps into confusion and devises new options; organizes what's messy.

Always -Sometimes -Never

THINKING TALENTS

Mentoring

"What can help others grow?"

Sees potential in others; every person is a work in progress; goal is to help others achieve success; searches for signs of growth in others.

Always -Sometimes -Never

THINKING TALENTS

Optimism

"What's right about this?"

Generous with praise; always on the lookout for the positive; contagiously enthusiastic; finds a way to lighten people's spirits. The glass is always half full.

Always -Sometimes -Never

THINKING TALENTS

Particularize

"How is each of us unique?"

Intrigued by unique qualities of each person; observes each person's style and how each thinks and builds relationships; keen observer and developer of others' talents and strengths.

Always -Sometimes -Never

THINKING TALENTS
Peacemaking

"Where is the common ground?"

Looks for areas of agreement; holds conflicts to a minimum; prefers to keep differences to a minimum and search for consensus; will modify own direction in service of harmony.

Always -Sometimes -Never

THINKING TALENTS
Precision

"How can I order this chaos?"

The world needs to be predictable; imposes structure, sets up routines, timelines, and deadlines; needs to feel in control; dislikes surprises, impatient with errors. Control is a way of maintaining progress and productivity.

Always -Sometimes -Never

THINKING TALENTS
Reliability

"How can I do this right?"

Excuses and rationalizations are not acceptable; has to take responsibility for anything committed to; reputation for conscientiousness and dependability. Easily frustrated by what is perceived as other's irresponsibility.

Always -Sometimes -Never

THINKING TALENTS
Seeking Excellence

"How can this be excellent?"

Excellence and efficiency is the measure—doing the best with the least. Everything—people, processes, products—is judged by how to make it better.

Always -Sometimes -Never

THINKING TALENTS
Standing Out

"How can I be recognized?"

Wants to be known for making a difference and be admired for credibility, success. Highly motivated by rewards and recognition programs.

Always -Sometimes -Never

THINKING TALENTS
Storytelling

"How can I bring these ideas to life with a story?"

Needs to explain by painting vivid pictures until others are inspired to act.

Always -Sometimes -Never

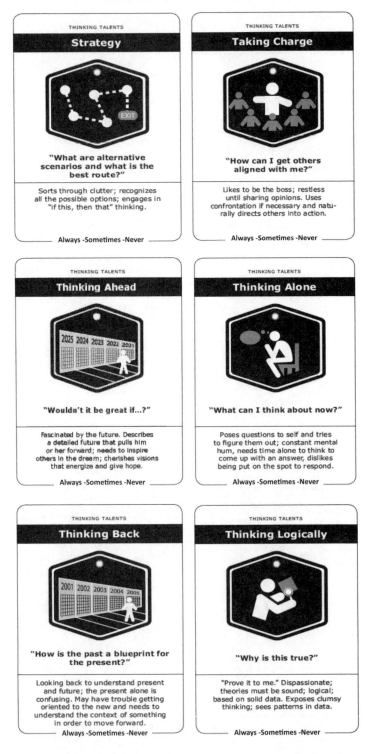

THINKING TALENTS

Strategy

"What are alternative scenarios and what is the best route?"

Sorts through clutter; recognizes all the possible options; engages in "if this, then that" thinking.

Always -Sometimes -Never

THINKING TALENTS

Taking Charge

"How can I get others aligned with me?"

Likes to be the boss; restless until sharing opinions. Uses confrontation if necessary and naturally directs others into action.

Always -Sometimes -Never

THINKING TALENTS

Thinking Ahead

"Wouldn't it be great if...?"

Fascinated by the future. Describes a detailed future that pulls him or her forward; needs to inspire others in the dream; cherishes visions that energize and give hope.

Always -Sometimes -Never

THINKING TALENTS

Thinking Alone

"What can I think about now?"

Poses questions to self and tries to figure them out; constant mental hum, needs time alone to think to come up with an answer, dislikes being put on the spot to respond.

Always -Sometimes -Never

THINKING TALENTS

Thinking Back

"How is the past a blueprint for the present?"

Looking back to understand present and future; the present alone is confusing. May have trouble getting oriented to the new and needs to understand the context of something in order to move forward.

Always -Sometimes -Never

THINKING TALENTS

Thinking Logically

"Why is this true?"

"Prove it to me." Dispassionate; theories must be sound; logical; based on solid data. Exposes clumsy thinking; sees patterns in data.

Always -Sometimes -Never

Right now you may be asking yourself some questions, such as: How do I use my thinking talents? How do they help me feel more understood? What does it mean that I don't have certain talents? Is there a negative side to the talents? We will address these questions thoroughly in the pages that follow. But rest assured that awareness of these talents will help increase your chances of reaching understanding.

What's Missing Is the Value of Hidden Talents

Valuing your thinking talents can sometimes be a challenge. Most of our thinking partners can reel off everything that's wrong with them, but they are confused when it comes to realizing the value of their cognitive assets. A man who worked with Angie discovered that Humor was a talent of his, but he shrugged and said, "What good is humor? People just think I'm a wise-ass. What's humor got to do with understanding anyhow?"

In our professional psychological training, our attention was continually directed toward what was wrong with people. Obviously this didn't help us discover how to grow health and sanity within and between people. It is no surprise, therefore, that self-criticism has become the norm.

It is our commitment to help people name, claim, and aim their innate talents in order to deepen their capacity to understand themselves and others and access the vitality and resources that are their birthright. To facilitate this, we created an additional way of recognizing the thinking talents that hide behind negative attributions. Some plants flourish in the sunshine and others prefer the shade, so we named these hidden, criticized, and untrained talents shadow attributes. They characteristically show up in an unconstructive way when a person is stressed, challenged, or struggling to make sense of something: "I am always so uptight about details!" "There I go again, being codependent." When the shadow attribute is recognized, however, you can learn to work with it, polish, and adjust it the way you would a rough diamond, allowing the light to shine through.

Consider these examples: Sarah was told since she was a child that she was impatient. She finally discovered that what was driving her was the thinking talent of Get to Action, used to excess. For years, Josh thought of himself as a loner, until he discovered that, in fact, his behavior was driven by the talent of Thinking Alone. Grace always adored being the center of attention at the office, but her friends described her as narcissistic; however, the thinking talent driving her behavior was Standing Out, which, when used well, won her several salesperson of the year awards. Steven's garage was so impeccably clean and organized that his neighbors jokingly called it the operating room. He had thought of himself as controlling until he came to understand that his behavior was being driven by his misunderstood thinking talent of Making Order.

How about you? Look at the list of shadow attributes below that correspond to each of the thinking talents. Do you recognize any talents you didn't choose in the first evaluation? What effect does it have on you to shift your perception from shadow to light?

CRITICISM/SHADOW ATTRIBUTE	THINKING TALENT
Wishy-washy	Adapting
Righteous	Believing
Overly loyal	Creating Intimacy
Hoarding	Collecting
Enmeshed in too many ideas or people	Connection
Pitchman	Enrolling
"It's not fair!"	Equalizing
Codependent	Feeling for Others
Critical	Fixing It
Obsessing on one thing	Focusing
Impatient	Get to Action
Driven	Goal Setting
Arrogant	Having Confidence
Wise-ass	Humor
Consulting everyone on everything	Including
"There must be a new way!"	Innovation
Learning junkie	Love of Learning
Pie in the sky	Loving Ideas
Controlling	Making Order
Preaching	Mentoring
Cheerleading	Optimism
Nosy	Particularize
Conflict-avoidant	Peacemaking
Nit-picking	Precision
Uptight	Reliability
Never satisfied	Seeking Excellence
Narcissist	Standing Out
Exaggerating	Storytelling
Scheming	Strategy
Bossy	Taking Charge
Crystal-ball gazing	Thinking Ahead
Loner	Thinking Alone
Stuck in the past	Thinking Back
Skeptical	Thinking Logically
Ruthless	Wanting to Win

What's Missing Is That Each Talent
Also Represents a Need

Every thinking talent also represents a particular need. When it is unmet, you can feel frustrated and misunderstood. When that need is recognized, the talent's potential can be realized and contribute to your understanding. Sheena, a client of Angie's, was trying to deal with a pessimistic new co-worker, Paul, whom she had been trying to cheer up every morning before team meetings. Upon reflection Sheena realized that her own thinking talent of Optimism was being eclipsed by trying to boost Paul's negative outlook. She was draining all her energy trying to buoy someone who likely needed another kind of mentoring. When Angie helped her recognize that her optimism needed to be valued and maintained, she asked another team member to talk through Paul's concerns and help him evaluate them.

As you review the following list of each talent and its associated need, notice which seem most relevant to you.

THINKING TALENT	WHAT DO I NEED TO UNDERSTAND AND FEEL UNDERSTOOD?
Adapting	A sense of flexibility and possibility for change as I approach a problem.
Believing	A strong presence of values.
Collecting	To know I can gather facts or acquire other things that support my understanding.
Connection	To find a bridge to another person or between ideas.
Creating Intimacy	To feel a sense of connection.
Enrolling	To seek and relate to unfamiliar people.
Equalizing	For things to feel fair.
Feeling for Others	To feel a sense of empathy for others as well as myself.
Fixing It	To enjoy my need to solve problems.
Focusing	To immerse myself in one thing at a time.

Get to Action	To know the tangible steps I can immediately take.
Goal Setting	To have a specific, clearly defined goal that I am moving toward.
Having Confidence	To enjoy trusting my own capacity.
Humor	To appreciate the ridiculous and absurd, in a light-hearted way.
Including	To consult with the others who are involved.
Innovation	To seek to realize new possibilities.
Love of Learning	To constantly reach for something new to learn in any given situation.
Loving Ideas	To explore new theories and models.
Making Order	To organize my thoughts and things in a way that makes sense to me.
Mentoring	To share my understandings with others and help them develop.
Optimism	To search for the bright and positive side of a situation.
Particularize	To observe and anticipate the specific needs of the people around me.
Peacemaking	To create harmony from diverse perspectives.
Precision	To be explicit with facts, actions, and word choices.
Reliability	To be accountable for the consequences of my actions and encourage others to do the same.
Seeking Excellence	To drive toward the best possible outcome that can be achieved.
Standing Out	To be recognized for making a difference.
Storytelling	To find meaning by linking experiences into a story.
Strategy	To explore all possible actions that can be taken in a situation.
Taking Charge	To direct my own and others' actions or thinking.
Thinking Ahead	To explore future possible outcomes.
Thinking Alone	To have introspective time alone to digest information and experiences.
Thinking Back	To reflect on what's happened in the past and how it informs the present.
Thinking Logically	To analyze specific facts and data of an issue.
Wanting to Win	To find a way to compete and surpass others.

Understanding what you actually need to think well can be liberating as well as exhilarating, as Dawna reveals in the following story:

> Jessica had recently married Steve and desperately wanted to be the most perfect wife she could be for him, but she was afraid she was not up to the task. When I asked her for one word to describe how she would know if she was "perfect," she replied without hesitation, "I'd be a refuge for him."
>
> Steve had been Jessica's lawyer for fifteen years, and he wanted to build an expansive new house so they could have a fresh start together. Jessica was overwhelmed and drained from attending to all the details that were entailed in building the house, and felt like she was continually letting Steve down.
>
> I helped her identify her thinking talents: Excellence, Feeling for Others, Connecting, Peacemaking, and Thinking Alone. It was obvious to us that Excellence was driving her need for perfection. Jessica realized she wasn't dragging her feet on each decision; she just needed lots of time to think through things on her own. She needed to understand the feelings of everyone involved, and make peace between them all so they could connect into a collaborative whole. And she needed to do all of that as excellently as possible.
>
> I asked her if she had ever been on a construction site where those conditions existed. Jessica looked off into space for a moment and then put her hand over her eyes, shook her head, and giggled. "No wonder I don't want to be involved! It is my worst nightmare—one frustration after another!" She looked away and then told me, "I could do it, Dawna, but I'd be so stressed and burned out that I'd be more like refuse than refuge to Steve. Which is exactly what I've been feeling since we began this project. I shudder every time the phone rings."
>
> A few days later, I helped Steve discover his thinking talents. We discovered that he needed to Take Charge, ensure Reliability, Make Order, and Think Logically and Strategically.

Supervising the building of a house met all those needs and energized him in the process.

Understanding this made it clear that he could meet his needs by taking over the building of the house. In stepping away from the day-to-day decision making, Jessica would be freed up, away from the job site, to create a refuge for Steve. She could use her talents for Feeling for Others, Connecting, and Peacemaking to support him in dealing with the tensions as they arose. What had first appeared to be an emotional and logistical misfit led to a true meeting of the best of their minds.

In the future, when you have a breakthrough in understanding, or have an experience that makes you feel fully alive, take a minute to reflect on which thinking talents you have just used. Pay attention to how your talents show up for you in different domains of life—work, exercise, family, hobbies—or with various people. This increased awareness will help you better engage each talent when you are relating to someone who thinks differently than you do.

WHAT'S MISSING IS COHERENCE

When you feel stuck in your thinking between different perspectives—"A part of me needs X, but another part needs Y" or "On the one hand I think B, but on the other I think D"—it can be because different thinking talents are not collaborating, as if one musical instrument wants to play the blues and the other Bach. It's also possible that, like Jessica, you don't have the thinking talents needed to understand "the big picture" and need to collaborate with someone who does.

The following process creates an internal coherence and align-ment that will enable you to access understanding.

- *Bring to mind a relational challenge you currently don't understand.*
- *Write each of your thinking talents down on a piece of paper.*
- *One by one, ask of each talent the following, as though it were a member of a council of wise advisers or a board of directors: "What guidance do you have for me in this challenge?" Let your hand write what comes to mind. Don't edit or overthink this. Write quickly, as if you are taking dictation.*
- *Get curious and wonder how you could implement what you have just been told.*
- *Acknowledge your council with gratitude, in a way that feels authentic, as you would if the guidance were coming from another person or external source.*

In the next chapter we'll illustrate how to use what you've learned about your own thinking talents to recognize and recon-cile the differences in understanding with someone else.

CHAPTER 5

Reconciling the Differences in the Ways We Understand

Out beyond ideas of wrongdoing and
rightdoing,
there is a field. I'll meet you there.

—Rumi

The very thing that has the most potential to separate us—that we each understand differently—has the most potential to connect us in a deeper way than we ever imagined. Indeed, our differences are what we have in common!

But how do you turn away from the walls of misunderstanding and toward the "field" that is beyond ideas of right and wrongdoing?

Reconciling with anyone you care about is filled with uncertainty. On some level, you always need to be ready to start again. In case you haven't noticed, however, your mind will do almost anything to avoid uncertainty, so this isn't easy. Yet if you succumb to this fear, you will keep repeating what hasn't worked in the past and proving to yourself that understanding isn't possible.

The two of us know this response to uncertainty on a cellular level. When we decided to write *Collaborative Intelligence: Thinking with People Who Think Differently*, we got lost within the first few days: We lost all sense of playfulness, surprise, curiosity. Angie understood what was needed to proceed in one way, Dawna in another. The two of us needed to invent new ways to navigate the differences in how each of us understands. Dawna had written thirteen books on her own and coauthored one with her husband, Andy, which almost destroyed their decades-long marriage. If she was going to write in collaboration with someone else, it had better be someone with a lot of passion, creativity, and perseverance. Angie had traveled the world, ridden on the back of an elephant that got attacked by a tiger, and taught two hundred deaf children who didn't understand English in rural Colombia, but the bulk of her writing experience had consisted of term papers and professional booklets. Was Dawna going to "teach" Angie? What would Angie do or say if Dawna got stuck? What if one of us understood something one way and the other another way? Angie had the robust energy of the prime of her life and Dawna the dwindling energy of her golden years. Separated by thousands of miles, three time zones, and the entire Pacific Ocean, how could we reconcile our differences to write the book without resentment, self-pity, or blame—the dirt in one pocket of all human beings?

The artist David Salle once said in an interview, "I have to get lost so I can invent some way out." And indeed, we knew we had to invent something; we weren't going to go forward in a straight line. Nothing natural or interesting goes in a straight line. What was not so apparent was that unless both of us became very curious about the way each of us understands something and recognized its value, we were headed toward relational disaster and the book would never grow between us. Where to start? We began by learning how to comfort our inner crocodiles.

Shifting from Crocodiles to Curiosity

In the last twenty-five years, research in the field of neuroscience has indicated that the human brain can grow beyond habit and increase its capacity for curiosity; it can learn to step back from the walls between you and another until you are curious enough to find out, metaphorically, what lies on the other's side, what he or she needs in order to understand.

In order to do that it's necessary to calm down your amygdala, a part of your brain that psychiatrist Dr. Seymour Boorstein calls the crocodile. Its function is fight or flee from those it considers a threat. It's not wise to soothe a crocodile by hugging it or trying to reason logically with it. But you can redirect its attention to the present moment so it can become curious enough to recognize it is not currently under attack.

Remember the practice of Reclaiming Your Attention that we shared in chapter 2 (see page 13)? By using it for three to four minutes, you will notice your breathing slowing and your awareness moving back toward your bodily sensations. Those two things indicate your mind is ready to get curious. Some people do this by going for a walk or taking a shower or in some other way taking a break from the stress or crisis at hand. Self-soothing in this way is the key to forestalling the crocodile's habitual fight-or-flight response and opening yourself to curiosity.

Which is exactly what each of us did in facing our first book collaboration. Once we got fiercely curious, we were freed from the prison of familiar ways of misunderstanding each other: "Who does she think she is, trying to boss me around!" or "Why does she keep wanting to understand the reasons for having to do it this way?" A larger acceptance than we had believed possible started opening up. We became willing to face and even embrace whatever stood between us: wounds from the past, sensitivities, and difficulties "hearing" each other. We were in that fresh and fertile open field.

From that place, we realized that we needed to stay curious about four things that would help us find the other on that field: what each of us needed to understand and how we expressed it; our blind spots; what the other needed to understand and how she expressed it; and how we could support each other to reconcile our differences.

Be Curious About Your Own Language of Understanding

How do you understand your own understanding? In our work with leadership teams, we had discovered that people needed a simple way to group their thinking talents in order to understand how to relate to one another while collaborating. To write the book, we decided to use a process we had been teaching those teams for eighteen years. It drew upon the ideas of Ned Herrmann, a thought leader in the field of brain dominance and author of *The Creative Brain*. He and Dawna had spoken many times about the role of intellectual diversity in growing human capacity.

Herrmann's model is based on more than 130,000 brain-dominance surveys (known as the "HBDI"). He proposed that there are four different preferred ways of knowing, understanding, and solving problems: analytic, procedural, relational, and innovative. According to Herrmann, people are born with the capacity to use all four, but as they mature, preferences are developed. Lives are shaped the way wind sculpts a tree, and you tend to develop particular preferences and avoidances when you want to understand something.

We think of these preferences as different languages of understanding, because they correlate so strongly with the language you use to understand a given situation: "Why?" (Analytic), "How?" (Procedural), "Who?" (Relational), and "What if . . . ?" (Innovative).

At every new intersection in writing our first coauthored book, Dawna would try to understand where to go next by asking, "What if we try this?" With that fundamental question, her mind was attempting to understand by innovating. Then she'd ask a relational question, perhaps checking out how Angie was feeling about the idea. Angie would then often ask her why the idea was so important—trying to understand by analyzing—and wonder how Dawna's new suggestion fit within the structure they had previously decided upon—a procedural inquiry if ever there was one. In the heat of experiencing our differences, we could more easily recognize those languages than stop to figure out which of our thinking talents were operating.

Based on Dawna's cognitive research, we have sorted the thirty-five thinking talents and arranged them into the appropriate Ned Herrmann quadrants. The result is the map of the four languages of understanding: analytic, procedural, innovative, and relational.

What languages of understanding do you prefer to use? You can use the map to find the language of each of your thinking talents. Then draw a four-square grid on a separate sheet of paper, to record what you have discovered. You will notice that there are four talents in the center column. We found that these talents could be used to understand in any of the four languages. You now have a map that reveals the language(s) you use most frequently to understand.

DRIVERS-OF-THINKING MAP

ANALYTIC
Concerned with data, facts, numbers, being "logical" and rational

INNOVATIVE
Concerned with the future, newness, possibilities, strategy, "big picture"

Talents in All Quadrants

Making Order
Organizing and aligning

Thinking Logically
Rational and data-focused

Innovation
New and different approaches

Loving Ideas
Looking for new theories, concepts

Seeking Excellence
Making the most of everything

Collecting
Acquiring things or facts

Love of Learning
Drawn to learn something new

Thinking Ahead
Always focused on the future

Wanting to Win
Inspired by competition

Fixing It
Seeing what's wrong, solving problems

Standing Out
Desiring recognition for success

Strategy
Finding alternate scenarios, options

Humor
Always finding humor in situations

Adapting
Flexible, doesn't mind change

Reliability
Responsible and accountable

Thinking Back
Using the past as a benchmark

Thinking Alone
Needing time to contemplate

Optimism
Positive enthusiasm

Including
"All for one, one for all"

Connection
Networking, building bridges

Get to Action
Making something happen now

Having Confidence
Self-assured

Creating Intimacy
Maintaining deep relationships

Peace-making
Seeking harmony

Enrolling
Creating new relationships

Focusing
Single-minded concentration

Equalizing
Fairness for everyone

Goal Setting
Constantly driven to accomplish

Storytelling
Using stories to inspire

Particularize
Observing and fostering uniqueness

Believing
Ethical, high values

Taking Charge
Directing others into action

Precision
Concerned with exactness

Mentoring
Fostering growth in others

Feeling for Others
Empathetic

PROCEDURAL
Concerned with process, operations, logistics, tactics

RELATIONAL
Concerned with feelings, morale, teamwork, development of people

LANGUAGES OF UNDERSTANDING

In the same way that some people understand only English and others may speak two or more languages, you may find that all of your thinking talents are clustered in one predominant quadrant of understanding or several. If they are mostly in the innovative quadrant, for example, it will be natural for you to come to understanding through ideas, seeking new approaches, and considering the future. If they're mostly in the procedural quadrant you will achieve understanding by considering logistics, time, details, and referencing the past. If your talents are mostly in the relational quadrant, you will naturally first consider feelings, people's needs, and how they are affected by decisions in the present. If you understand primarily through analytic thinking, you will naturally want to consider why a misunderstanding exists in the first place, break down the reasons, and think about how often it occurs in the present. All of these signify very different perspectives on the same issue.

Most of us are "multilingual": We have two or more languages of understanding, that is, analytic and procedural or innovative and relational. If, for example, your thinking talents are Taking Charge, Precision, Focusing, Mentoring, Including, and Optimism, you will use both the relational and procedural languages of understanding. You will need a clear process and be highly attuned to the effect on others.

Having thinking talents clustered in different quadrants is quite common and explains why so many people feel divided in their thinking. Herrmann's findings showed that 7 percent of adults have just one preference; 60 percent favor two; 30 percent favor three; and just 3 percent have equal preferences for all four styles.

If your thinking talents are clustered in two quadrants, you may constantly feel pulled in opposing directions because you're considering understanding something from two perspectives at the same time. For example, "I need to analyze why it matters, at the

same time, I need to seek new possibilities and try something new."
This is analytic understanding and innovative understanding trying to reconcile. Or you may hear yourself thinking, On the one
hand I need to have a plan and tangible next steps, yet on the other
hand I need to know the effect of my choices on my family. This is
procedural understanding and relational understanding trying to
reconcile.

If all of your talents are in one quadrant, you may have developed focused mastery in this language of understanding, but you
will therefore probably be confused by disagreement from someone who understands from another quadrant.

For example, Joan, a thinking partner of ours, had all of her
thinking talents in the procedural quadrant. She was an organizational genius who minimized risks whenever possible and moved
through her life taking one predictable step after another. She was
very much in control of her actions and seemed to be very sure of
herself. But when someone at work brought up financial consider-
ations, discussed feelings, or jumped in with a new idea, she shut
down their input as quickly as she could. She never had to deal
with reconciling differences in understanding inside of her own
well-oiled, one-way process of understanding and thus was un-
practiced doing it outside her own skin.

If your thinking talents fall into all four quadrants, you may
find that understanding is like directing an orchestra. This can feel
chaotic. To bring out your best thinking, you may need more time
to come to decisions, because you are considering things from so
many different perspectives. It also can be extremely valuable because when you take the time to reconcile those different ways of
understanding within your own mind, you have the capacity to do
it outside of you as well.

Be Curious About Your Blind Spots

Are there one or more quadrants in the map where you have no thinking talents? We call this a blind spot. Don't worry—there's nothing wrong with you and you are not alone. No one has all thirty-five of the talents; there is always some specific perspective that is missing.

For example, all of Dawna's thinking talents are in the innovative and relational quadrants. She therefore has two blind spots—analytic and procedural. Angie on the other hand has thinking talents in all four quadrants; therefore, she has no blind spots (but this doesn't mean she has all the talents or never gets stuck, as you will soon see).

When you have a blind spot, it's easy to devalue that particular kind of thinking and even brush it off as unneeded. You may habitually try to convince or make the other person see things using your own language of understanding. In our case, when we came to an issue where we were stuck, Dawna tried to share her thoughts by coming up with metaphors or a wild new idea to explain a theory (innovative understanding). If Angie responded analytically by suggesting we first step back and understand the issue, her well-intended words bounced off like water on a windshield. Dawna wanted to get back to innovative thinking: "Yes, but . . . Yes, but . . ." she'd say. If we hadn't learned to recognize each other's language of understanding we could have been forever stuck in this unproductive mode of communication. But Angie did come to understand that Dawna needed to offer her new ideas, and Dawna understood that Angie was trying to help her analyze which ideas were the most effective.

It's worth noting that people tend to worry and stress in their blind spots. You intuitively trust you will be able to understand something when you are thinking from your energizing talents. But if you think about an issue from a quadrant where you have no thinking talents, your brain burns out quickly. If you don't have Feeling for Others as an example, you may worry about how people will react to you. If you don't have Making Order, you may frequently worry about prioritizing and organizing.

Two common assumptions cause us to deny our blind spots. The first is that we should be competent at everything. We often, therefore, try to hide our blind spots so that we don't appear inadequate. The second is that we should be able to understand an issue completely on our own. Both of these assumptions are erroneous and limit us. Blind spots reveal where people need each other and how we can give and receive support to reach understanding.

You may have been taught to believe that having to ask for support means you are not self-sufficient. If, on the other hand, you recognize a blind spot and use it as an opportunity to ask for help from a person who is energized by understanding in this way, the relational intelligence between the two of you can grow. Without Angie's procedural and analytic ways of understanding, you would not be reading these pages, as you will see in the next section. Without Dawna's thinking talents to support Angie, there would also be no stories and far fewer new ideas.

Be Curious About the Other's Language of Understanding

It is much easier to recognize someone else's language of understanding than it is to pick out their specific thinking talents moment to moment in the midst of conversation. Bring to mind someone in your life you currently don't understand as well as you'd like to. Listen to them with curiosity when they are trying to convince you about something. Considering the map below of the four languages, what kind of thinking do they use most frequently when they want you to understand their point of view? Be curious about which quadrant(s) their thinking is coming from.

LANGUAGES OF UNDERSTANDING

ANALYTIC	INNOVATIVE
Understands through data, facts, and numbers, being "logical" and rational	Understands by looking at future, newness, possibilities, strategy, and big picture
PROCEDURAL	**RELATIONAL**
Understands through processes, the past, logistics, and timelines	Understands through feelings, morale, collaboration, and development of people

A thinking partner of ours, Paul, was a master communicator at work, but complained that he and his fourteen-year-old daughter, Mandy, didn't understand each other at all. "I want to know more about her life, but when I ask her what's going on, she just rolls her eyes and folds her arms across her chest."

"Give us an example of a time when she did talk to you," we asked. As he spoke, we plotted Mandy's comments according to which language of understanding she was speaking from.

"She told me about how much fun she had with her friends at the football game and how devastated she was when the guy she really liked, Dave, ignored her completely."

"Which quadrant is that—analytic, procedural, innovative, or relational?" Angie asked.

"Okay. Well, she's talking about 'who' and her feelings so I guess that's relational?" As Angie wrote Mandy's name in that quadrant, Dawna asked Paul how he'd responded to Mandy.

"I asked her why she felt that way. I pointed out to her that she had wasted four hours of a Saturday morning on someone who wasn't worth her time."

When we asked him to try to identify from which quadrant he had been trying to understand, he stared into space and then answered, "Obviously I was asking 'Why?' and trying to convince her to analyze the value she received from the amount of time spent on that jerk. It's all analytic, isn't it?" Angie wrote his name in the upper left quadrant and asked him how he might have responded differently if the conversation had been with a customer at work.

"Well, I'd just tell him that I was sorry he had had such a lousy time and ask if there was anything I could do to help." Angie now wrote Paul's name in the lower right relational quadrant.

Upon seeing the way his and Mandy's languages of understanding were laying out, he got excited: "Of course! It's so obvious. If I want her to know I understand her, I have to speak her language, at least at first. Then maybe I'll stand a chance of bringing her around to my way of understanding."

It does seem so obvious when it's someone else, doesn't it?

Without awareness, most people like Paul give counsel in language that helps *them* understand but not necessarily the other person. This approach makes the other feel misunderstood. When instead you discover someone else's language, as Paul came to do for Mandy, and begin to talk from there, you have come a long way toward making connection for reconciliation.

Be Curious About How You Can Reconcile Differences in Understanding

Our culture celebrates the rugged individualist (Indiana Jones, Han Solo, Lara Croft—you get the idea) and rewards people who can pull themselves up by their bootstraps without help. The message behind this is that the less you rely on others, the better off you'll be. But it is a delusion to think that we can get through life on our own. At the heart of understanding is the choice to turn toward one another and recognize what theologian Thomas Merton called "our hidden wholeness." In other words, what is awake in you is dormant in me and I need you to awaken it in me. And vice versa. We are interdependent. It is as obvious as a violin needing a bow to play.

When the two of us circled each of our thinking talents on one map, we could quickly see both our differences in understanding. It also became obvious how we could be resources to each other and the light that Angie brings to Dawna's blind spots and vice versa. When Dawna saw Angie's need for Get to Action as a talent instead of impatience, her worries about being able to finish the book were eased. When Angie realized Dawna's "preaching" was in fact the talent of Mentoring, she could grow from her suggestions. As we made these seemingly small shifts in perception the door opened, and we could discover new ways of supporting each other and to be supported.

The talents we have in common are: Innovation, Loving Ideas, Strategy, and Seeking Excellence. This meant that when dreaming up what we wanted this book to say, creating strategies for how we could write it (even when separated by an entire ocean), filling it with new ideas, finding new ways to actualize those ideas, and revising ad infinitum until it was as close to excellent as we could make it, we were completely aligned and in harmony.

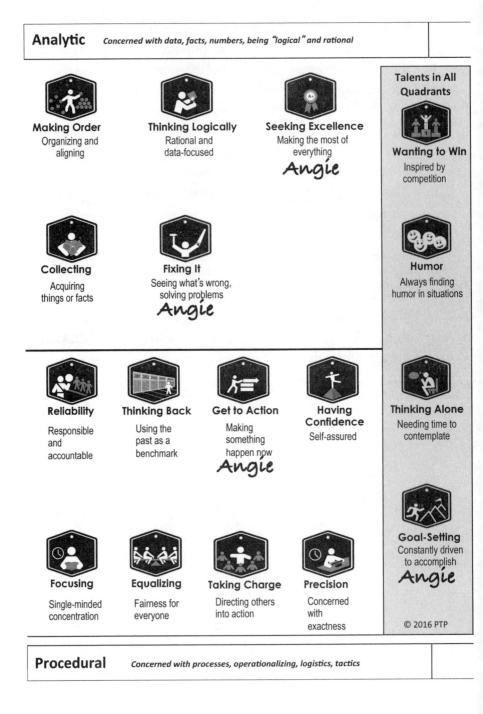

Analytic   *Concerned with data, facts, numbers, being "logical" and rational*

Making Order
Organizing and
aligning

Thinking Logically
Rational and
data-focused

Seeking Excellence
Making the most of
everything
Angie

Talents in All Quadrants

Wanting to Win
Inspired by
competition

Collecting
Acquiring
things or facts

Fixing It
Seeing what's wrong,
solving problems
Angie

Humor
Always finding
humor in situations

Reliability
Responsible
and
accountable

Thinking Back
Using the
past as a
benchmark

Get to Action
Making
something
happen now
Angie

Having Confidence
Self-assured

Thinking Alone
Needing time to
contemplate

Focusing
Single-minded
concentration

Equalizing
Fairness for
everyone

Taking Charge
Directing others
into action

Precision
Concerned
with
exactness

Goal-Setting
Constantly driven
to accomplish
Angie

© 2016 PTP

Procedural   *Concerned with processes, operationalizing, logistics, tactics*

Concerned with future, newness, possibilities, strategy, big picture   **Innovative**

Innovation
New and
different
approaches
Dawna
Angie

Loving Ideas
Looking for new
theories,
concepts
Dawna
Angie

Love of Learning
Drawn to learn
something new

Thinking Ahead
Always focused on
the future
Dawna

Standing Out
Desiring
recognition for
success

Strategy
Finding alternate
scenarios, options
Angie
Dawna

Adapting
Flexible,
doesn't mind
change

Optimism
Positive
Dawna

Including
"All for one, one
for all."

Connection
Networking, building
bridges
Dawna

Creating Intimacy
Maintaining deep
relationships

Peacemaking
Seeking harmony

Enrolling
Creating new
relationships

Storytelling
Using stories to
inspire
Dawna

Particularizing
Observing
and fostering
uniqueness

Believing
Ethical, high
values

Mentoring
Fostering growth
in others
Dawna

Feeling for Others
Empathetic
Angie

Concerned with feelings, morale, teamwork, development of people   **Relational**

———

The following stories illustrate how thinking partners of ours learned to reconcile their different ways of understanding in four different situations: giving advice, dealing with time and money, responding to stress, and expressing intimacy. We chose these because they illustrate common issues where misunderstandings can show up.

Reconciling Different Ways of Understanding

"I DON'T UNDERSTAND HOW I CAN HELP YOU"

When Meredith offers advice to her brother, Steve, about how to do his philosophy term paper, he bristles. Since Meredith has four analytic talents and one relational—Mentoring—she naturally wants to help him understand why he is stuck. Steve has all relational talents and resents the way Meredith just jumps in to tell him why he should approach his paper in a more logical way.

Angie helped Meredith map out their differences so she could analyze why it would be most effective to first ask Steve how he feels about his paper. If he feels understood, she can then offer advice and become a resource to him by offering help in creating an analytic structure. If he's not open to help at that time, she can tell him she is available whenever he needs support. In any case, she could ask *him* for help with her social life.

Here are the general characteristics of the four languages of understanding as applicable to giving advice. The bullet points in a quadrant will help you recognize when someone is coming from that particular perspective. Knowing this helps you realize what the other person has to offer and deepen your understanding of them.

GIVING ADVICE FROM EACH PERSPECTIVE

ANALYTIC	INNOVATIVE
• "Why are you letting this bother you? It's not such a big deal." • "You're thinking about this the wrong way." • "Let's break the problem down and look at this logically." • "This is happening because . . ."	• "I've got a lot of ideas for you. Have you thought of . . ." • "It's hard now, but look ahead to where you'll be six months from now." • "I just learned something new that could really help you . . ." • "Let's strategize about what your options are."
PROCEDURAL	**RELATIONAL**
• "Walk me back through the problem—give me the details of what happened." • "You need to take it step-by-step and focus on one thing at a time." • "The responsible thing to do is . . ." • "What precisely is the problem?"	• "Oh, you poor thing, that sounds hard, how can I help?" • "Of course you feel that way . . ." • "I know you'll get past this; just think of all the people who care about you." • "I think you need to talk to this person and air your feelings."

"WHAT IS OUR TRUE WEALTH?"

Malcolm feels deflated by the way his partner, John, manages their spending. Every time Malcolm proposes a great new idea that he's excited about implementing in their apartment, John responds by asking, "But where will we find the money?" Malcolm has innovative and relational thinking talents. John, as you may have guessed, understands through his procedural and analytic talents.

Dawna mapped out their differences. Malcolm immediately recognized the value that John brought to the relationship—he kept them in the black and paid bills on time. It was a little more difficult for John to see the value of Malcolm's creative spirit. To move beyond feeling controlled, he needed to practice Reclaiming Your Attention until he was curious and could genuinely listen to his partner's ideas. At first it was about as easy as learning to eat with chopsticks, but understanding the value each's thinking brought to the other made it both energizing and worthwhile.

Below are the characteristics of each of the four languages of understanding as they show up in common issues of time and money. Discovering where each person's thinking is coming from minimizes the chances of a breakdown and maximizes empathy for the other.

MANAGING TIME AND MONEY FROM EACH PERSPECTIVE

ANALYTIC	INNOVATIVE
• Tries to maximize every dollar and researches the best deals • Carefully considers pros/cons of a purchase • Needs to know current financial status • Oriented to the present, doesn't want to waste time	• Measures value by what is learned • Possible benefits override cost • Likes to spend time and money on what's new • Likes to find ways to generate money rather than save • Focused on what's "next," already living in the future in his/her mind
PROCEDURAL	**RELATIONAL**
• Interested in saving money • Sets and keeps budgets • Looks to the past to prevent mistakes from reoccurring • Likes to revisit history in order to understand the context of what's happening now • Aware of and tracks how long something takes	• Enjoyment is more important than cost • Likes spending on social events and helping people • Loves to give gifts and tips well • Time is not as important as being there for each other • Prioritizes people's needs and feelings over schedules

"THIS STRESSES ME OUT!"

When Bode gets talking about his dreams for a new career, he gets excited and it seems as if he might launch in his new direction immediately! The way he jumps to conclusions and makes rapid-fire "plans" leaves his girlfriend, Meghan, feeling left out completely from his future. Her response is to withdraw from his musings or get very upset. Convinced that Bode doesn't really think about how she might fit into his newly imagined future, she either fights with him about it or freezes.

Angie charted their different ways of understanding and the analysis was very enlightening to both of them. It revealed that Bode has five talents in the innovative quadrant and two in procedural. It was natural for him to try to understand their future direction by thinking about one idea after another and figure out how their past could guide their future. Because Meghan has four relational talents and three analytic, she explained that what she needed was for Bode to consider her way of understanding by asking her how she would feel about each option and then listening to why it matters to her.

Each person relates to stress differently. Below are the characteristics of each of the four languages of understanding as they show up in stressful situations. Discovering where each person's thinking is coming from will help you relate to the other's stress and grow compassion between you.

RELATING TO STRESSFUL SITUATIONS FROM EACH PERSPECTIVE

ANALYTIC	INNOVATIVE
• Can get stuck on analyzing pros and cons • May have difficulty proceeding until reasoning is understood • Keeps wanting more data, but there is never enough • Paralysis by analysis	• Can get stuck on several ideas at the same time • May be extremely frustrated with how long things take to enact • Throws out as many ideas as possible; any new idea is better than not doing anything • Paralysis by too many ideas
PROCEDURAL	RELATIONAL
• Can get stuck in the way it's been in the past • May get rigid and resistant to change • Wants everything to stay the same • Paralysis by regimentation	• Can get overwhelmed by the feelings of others • Need to withdraw may get intensified • Trouble overriding feelings and just moving on • Paralysis by emotion

"HOW DO I LOVE YOU? LET ME COUNT THE WAYS"

Sara complains to Dawna that she's ready to leave her husband, Joe, because she's sure he doesn't love her. She insists that even though she's asked him to go to counseling with her, he insists he's just too busy. She interprets his busyness as a lack of commitment to their romance. She admits that intimacy without romance just doesn't turn her on.

Joe agrees to analyze their thinking talents for the sake of finding mutual understanding. They discover that Sara has five relational thinking talents and two innovative ones. No wonder she needs to feel an emotional connection and wants to create closeness by trying new things together. The map reveals that Joe, on the other hand, has all of his thinking talents in the procedural quadrant. He feels most comfortable when he is doing what he has always done. Romance and novelty are a language he just doesn't speak.

Dawna explains that research indicates that the human brain can grow from new experiences. She suggests that Joe schedule one romantic night a week on his calendar, and that Sara design what happens on that night. They both agree that if, after two months, this doesn't work for them, they will interview counselors together until they find one who thinks relationally and procedurally.

People often have misunderstandings and hurt feelings because they miss the unique ways a spouse or partner expresses love and affection. Below are the characteristics of the four languages of understanding as they show up when expressing intimacy. Discovering where each person is coming from will help you avoid misunderstandings and recognize the other's expressions of love.

EXPRESSING INTIMACY FROM EACH PERSPECTIVE

ANALYTIC	INNOVATIVE
• Tries to get close by talking about what is and isn't working • In intimate situations analyzes and reasons what's going on in the moment: "Well, if we had sex now, it would be rushed, because guests are arriving. But if I wait until later, I will be too tired . . ." • Loves to have his/her reasons received without criticism	• Likes to try new things, and have fresh experiences. Ranges from sexual experimentation to a new location or type of date: "Tonight I want to do something different. I learned about a new very romantic restaurant that serves Mongolian food." • Loves to have his/her ideas received without criticism

PROCEDURAL	RELATIONAL
• Likes to have scheduled intimacy, and enjoys comfort of routine, whether sexual or for romantic dates • "We can go to our favorite restaurant and still have time to go upstairs before the kids come home" • Loves to have his/her plan received without criticism	• Likes to have experiences that lead to a strong sense of connection. Prefers intense emotional connection to have a sexual connection: "It feels so good to be close to you. I love sharing these moments with you." • Loves to have his/her feelings received without criticism

Mutual understanding between you and another person depends upon uncovering the value each of you brings to the thinking. When you learn to recognize and appreciate the innate talents of those most important to you, it can help release energy and aliveness between you. We invite you to re-create the map on pages 110–111 on a separate piece of paper and chart yourself and another person you have trouble understanding (or who has trouble understanding you). Consider these questions: What are each of your languages of understanding? What are each of your blind spots? What would be the most effective way to communicate this to each other?

When people look at their maps, we often hear comments like: "Oh, so *that's* why she . . ." "I never thought of his *x* as a talent!" "I wish I had known this when we were arguing . . ." Understanding these differences will reveal how specifically you can help each other and bridge your perspectives.

Our differences are what we have in common. Each of us has a unique purpose. We are all instruments in a giant orchestra. The way each of us plays affects the rest of us. Your individual actions matter. Every moment is an opportunity to discover this.

In the last two chapters, you've been discovering differences in understanding. We offer you the following practice of curiosity to discover commonalities.

You are invited to go for a brief walk in a relatively crowded place. As you pass people, consider them fellow travelers on a learning journey, experiencing life together with you. For a few minutes, silently wish them safety, satisfaction, and connection with those they love.

Notice the effect of this in your body, your mind, your overall sense of connection and well-being.

In the next section of this book, you'll learn how to recognize and reconcile the differences in how each of you solves problems.

Discovery Three:

LEARN

Different Ways of Learning—Through the
Discovery of Inquiry Styles

CHAPTER 6

Mapping the Way
You Learn

*It is, in fact, nothing short of a miracle that the modern
methods of instruction have not yet entirely strangled
the holy curiosity of inquiry.*

—Albert Einstein

What do you know about how you learn? What are the conditions
that maximize your learning and what minimizes it? What is different about the way that you learn and the way that a particular
person you care about learns?

Learning as a concept, whether in math, language, engineering,
or athletics, is usually associated with adding information or capabilities to your repertoire. When it comes to relating to others, we
think of learning as discovering something is possible. As you've
read in previous chapters, when people think they have irreconcilable differences, they are saying, in essence, that they communicate and understand in different ways. They are also saying that
they don't know how to learn with each other and therefore, nothing can be possible between them. The other side of that coin is
that when two people reconcile their different ways of learning,
they discover what can be possible between them.

All learning begins with a question that pries the fist of your mind open. If you think of a young child beginning to walk, you'll recognize that the way the human mind learns is by inquiring, exploring, moving forward, falling, inquiring, reaching, moving forward, falling, inquiring. The falling is never a failure, just part of the process of learning.

If you think of an acorn, you'll realize that it bears within its small shell the potential of a huge oak tree asking to be lived. In order for that potential to be realized, that shell, which protected the acorn for so long, has to break open. The breaking open is not a failure. It is part of the process of letting go of what is no longer needed, so a bigger self can emerge. The potential that learning evokes isn't an abstract concept. It is an imperative you feel from the inside out. It is what naturally causes you to reach toward another and into the larger world. Without it, you have no way of discovering the importance of your life. Learning encourages you to open and reach, questing as a seed does.

Neuroscientists have developed a new paradigm over the past twenty-five years since discovering that the brain is highly plastic. We now understand that it rewires itself in response to experience and relationships. It continues to change as your environment, experiences, and the ways you relate change. This enables you to learn, unlearn, and relearn throughout your life. On the other hand, if you are stuck in certainty and not learning, the circuits in your brain will become fixed, and you will keep repeating the same crazy actions over and over. You diminish or expand your life according to how you think about your capacity to learn.

Most adults today have been educated under a different paradigm. You were told to quest for certainty, to reach for the right answer. You were trained to develop mastery, to solve problems, to "decide"—a word that has the Latin root -*cide*, which means to kill (as in suicide, fratricide, etc.). So, in deciding you kill off all possibilities until you find the right one. Think of your mind as a hand that reaches, grabs something it is told is valuable, and holds on to it. When you hold enough correct answers, your mind has mastered a skill or a profession, a good grade or promotion. As you develop, that hand stops reaching because it is so busy holding on to all it has grasped. It may feel as though you have mastered the task at hand, but the moment you metaphorically shut your fist, you have stopped learning.

We worked with Paul, a CEO, and his CTO, Marlene, on this very problem. Paul had his hands full. He had worked hard in one of the top ten business schools in the world. He could answer any question anyone asked him. His leadership team followed his lead, and his wife quickly learned to follow suit. A conversation between any of them was like a tennis game of slamming one certainty after another back and forth over a net of confusion. Paul loved the excitement of "winning" those conversations, because he was more certain than anyone else and made sure they all knew it. But when he tried to engage Marlene in this way, she did something very different, something true to her nature. She asked him one question after another: "Why do you think that?" "What if there's another way to look at this situation?" "What about the possibility that . . ." "Has anyone ever done it differently?" This drove Paul crazy. He'd fold his arms tighter and tighter across his chest until it seemed as if he wasn't even breathing whenever she'd speak. Privately, he told us he had decided to fire Marlene because she was "weak." When we asked him for the data he had used to draw this conclusion, he replied emphatically that anyone who asked questions, and so many questions, and questions that couldn't really be answered anyway, was weak.

Paul was hardwired to achieve mastery. He had been trained to decide; his brain had been trained to kill off all possibilities except one as soon as possible. This is called converging. Many of the questions Marlene asked required his brain to do exactly the opposite, to diverge, to begin to open into what is commonly called confusion. Needless to say, Paul and most of his leadership team were very uncomfortable with confusion.

Most of us are, as a matter of fact. If you want attention, just tell someone you know that you are confused. Inevitably they will try to help you converge—to clear up confusion—and decide on the right thing to do or say. But confusion is as natural to the human mind as a tide is to the ocean. It's a sign that the brain is opening to learn how to digest new information or a new perspective with what you already know. Since you've been trained to "fix" confusion whenever possible by closing down possibilities, confusion is the place where learning stops and possibilities are killed off.

We are definitely hardwired to quest for mastery, but we are also hardwired to learn, to explore the mystery of what we don't know. The two explorations require very different kinds of questions. In the latter, your hand reaches, it stays open, exploring what connections can be possible. Think of two jazz musicians tuning their own instruments and then reaching in the quest to connect with the other in a new harmony. Think of members of a choir singing within their different ranges while questing to create a coherent sound with the others. The mind doesn't "find" the one right way and close on it. It opens further and further, searching, learning, finding, losing, finding in a new way.

In chapter 5 you discovered your thinking talents and which ones clustered to become your language of understanding—analytic, procedural, innovative, or relational. Now we will explore how these quadrants mirror your inquiry style—the kinds of questions you naturally prefer and ask yourself in order to learn.

In this chapter, you will map your inquiry style and then learn several ways you can use it to quest more deeply into your own wisdom and potential. In the next chapter, you will discover how to reconcile the differences in the ways you and another learn.

What Is Your Inquiry Style?

Our professional experience has led us to recognize that each person prefers to learn by using a particular kind of inquiry, a favored type of question that seems natural to them, in the same way that a language of understanding does. Your inquiry style is the way you naturally explore an issue when you are confused. Pinpointing that style is the key to understanding your particular bias for working through new-to-you information or capabilities. The four different inquiry styles:

- Analytic: You ask questions about "why?"
- Procedural: You ask questions about "how?"
- Relational: You ask questions about "who?"
- Innovative: You ask questions about "what if?"

ANALYTIC INQUIRY: THE "WHY?"

- If you naturally gravitate toward analytic inquiry, you have an affinity for asking questions about fixing and arranging. "Why is this true?" "What are the facts?" "What does the data indicate?" "What is the most logical way to approach this?"
- You also have an affinity for clarifying and quantifying by pulling an idea or problem apart in order to comprehend it, to focus on making things excellent.

PROCEDURAL INQUIRY: THE "HOW?"

- If your mind asks "how" questions, your inquiry style is procedural. You have an affinity for questions about planning, step-by-step process, and gauging how long things will take. "How will we do this?" "How much time will it take?" "What's the deadline?"
- You have an affinity for inquiring about the sequencing of events, history, and context.
- You tend to inquire about priorities and the end result so that it will be predictable and repeatable.

RELATIONAL INQUIRY: THE "WHO?"

- If you naturally wonder about the feelings and needs of others, and how a situation will affect people—you have an affinity for relational inquiry. "How do you feel about that?" "Who could help you?" "What kind of support do you need?"
- You will tend to ask questions about the quality of relationships and how to help yourself and others grow and develop.

INNOVATIVE INQUIRY: THE "WHAT IF?"

- If you have an affinity for innovative inquiry, you inquire about new ideas, concepts, and inventive ways of working. "What could we do that no one's ever done before?" "What are all the ways we could approach this?" "What's our vision?"
- You naturally ask questions that explore the most imaginative possibilities and draw others into the future.
- You often inquire about underlying patterns and combine different ideas and concepts into something creative.

To make it easier for you to see and compare the different styles we have organized them into four quadrants.

INQUIRY STYLES

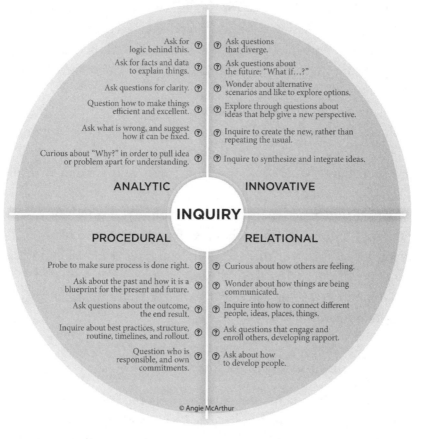

© Angie McArthur

Questions about How You Ask Questions

HOW DO I RECOGNIZE MY INQUIRY STYLE?

The kind of questioning you favor becomes your inquiry style, the default setting that you use to navigate learning. Notice in the illustration above where your questions naturally orient. Mark the quadrant(s) you use most often with a star. Do you automatically want to know "why" the problem exists? Or are you more interested in "who" the problem impacts? Do you have a tendency to start with questions to generate ideas? Or isn't there enough time to do this?

Another interesting way to discover your inquiry style is to just begin to make a list of all the questions on your mind, one by one, such as "What will I have for dinner? Where are my kids? How will I resolve the issues with my sister?" etc. Keep going as quickly as possible, number as you go, and continue until there are at least fifty. This may feel like a relief because you no longer have to carry them tangled in your mind.

Using the inquiry style quadrants as a guide, go through your list and label each according to the type of question it is. For example, "What will I have for dinner?" and "Where are my kids?" are procedural, whereas "How will I resolve the issues with my sister?" is relational.

Given this quick snapshot, what would you now say is your preferred inquiry style? In the next few days, you're likely to be much more aware of the questions you have a tendency to ask. You may discover that these fifty were not representative of your usual inquiry style, or you may clearly recognize the same style as you found here.

HOW DO I WORK WITH INQUIRY STYLES?

Your inquiry style helps you trust yourself and feel more confident when solving an issue: "As long as I have a plan, I can learn anything!" "As long as I know how the other person feels, I trust I can learn my way through this." "As long as I can figure out what is wrong, I can move forward." "As long as I can think about new options, I trust I'll learn my way through this."

You can also use the quadrant illustration as a tool to guide you through recognizing the style(s) of inquiry that is *not* native to you. You can think of these unfamiliar ways of asking questions as your inquiry blind spots because you usually ignore them or you might even react adversely to them. Recognizing these nonhabitual questions can open a whole new landscape for you to explore. They encourage you to climb a little higher, go a little further, dig a little deeper than you usually do.

Considering different kinds of questions will widen your perspective and help you learn in unexpected ways. Imagine you are standing at the edge of the Grand Canyon with a brown paper bag on your head. Let's pretend you've worn it for so long that it feels natural. It has two pinholes through which you view everything and everyone. The bag represents your current limited perception of yourself and another person. All that's needed to liberate your view of the world is a simple nonhabitual question such as, "What happens if I take off this bag?" Suddenly, you will realize that there is more to the world than you previously thought.

WHAT GETS IN THE WAY OF YOUR LEARNING?

Just as there is a shadow side to your thinking talents, there is also a shadow side to each of the inquiry styles. Your shadow style is an additional way of recognizing questions that are expressed negatively or unconstructively and usually show up (are expressed) when you are stressed, challenged, or struggling to make sense of something. You might think of them as negative self-talk. For example: "Why am I always so rigid about timing!" "Can I ever stop being needy?" The shadow sides of your inquiry style hide in the dark of your confusion when you are relating to pain, fear, or stressful challenges. They have the effect of closing your mind to new possibilities. Just like the shadow side of thinking talents, as soon as you recognize these shadow questions, you can uncover the light beneath them. The following illustration will help you identify your habitual shadow questions.

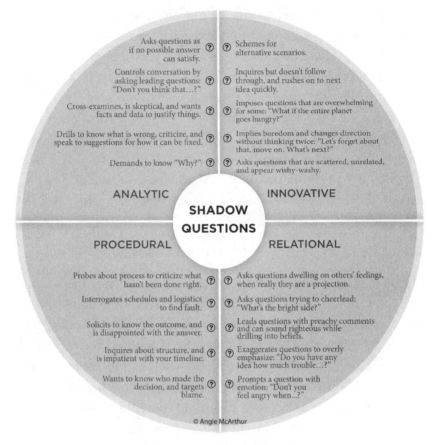

What this illustration reveals is how shadow questions block you from using your inquiry style. For example, if you have been cross-examining yourself in a critical way, the illustration shows that you are actually trying to inquire analytically. If you constantly ask yourself about other people's feelings, you're in fact attempting to inquire relationally.

If you are pelting yourself or someone with shadow questions, consider a more effective way to open your mind so you can learn. Ask yourself, What is important to me about this question? This will loosen your mind enough to find a more skillful way of asking a question from that quadrant. Doing so, you will inquire as an ally rather than an antagonist.

Hanging by a Thread

Angie shares a story about how an injured athlete used inquiry to learn.

> I was talking to Mark about his visit to his doctor earlier in the day. Clearly the news wasn't good and he was frustrated. He gazed for several minutes over my shoulder at a horizon I couldn't see before telling me what was going on.
>
> "I have no idea what the problem with my back is or what to do about it. All I know is that I've seen three doctors in two weeks, had nine procedures in four months, and nothing's any better. I don't know where to go from here." His voice sounded hollow as he continued, "To top it all off, I just came from having lunch with my sister Elena, who's always been my main support. This time I came away feeling even worse. All she did was fire one question after another at me. I couldn't answer any of them: 'Why can't the doctors figure it out? How many more physical therapy sessions will your insurance cover? Have you researched all the options? Why don't you get a second opinion? Why are you taking painkillers when you know there are dangerous side effects?' "
>
> His jaw muscles tightened and his voice flattened, as he went on, "What does she want from me? I have untreatable back pain. In a week, I'm having another surgery on my shoulder, followed by a massive medical bill to top it all off. What planet is Elena on? How can she be so clueless? Why can't she just feel how hard this all is for me?
>
> "That's why I'm asking you to help me, Angie. I feel like I'm hanging by a thread here—just like my back is!" He pulled himself out of the chair and paced angrily in front of the window.
>
> At first, all I could offer was presence and silence. It was difficult to see Mark so vulnerable. I did know two things, though: First, there was some way this could be an opportunity for him and his sister to actually get closer to each other. Sec-

ond, that Mark could learn how to ask questions that would help him access his own inner wisdom in order to relate differently to both his body and his sister. I suggested a practice he could do by himself, which we could discuss afterward. He wasn't eager, but he was willing. "I guess so. I feel completely helpless, so I'm willing to try anything."

I described the Solo Clearness Committee process and placed both the inquiry quadrant illustration and the shadow questions on the table in front of him. He scribbled furiously for twenty minutes. The blank sheet of paper filled with doodles, expletives, explanations, and insights. Finally, he leaned back in the chair and released a long sigh. "I know there's not much I can do about the condition of my back. That's up to the surgeon for now, but what this helped me realize is that I've been asking myself the wrong questions about the wrong things, and so has my sister."

He pushed himself out of the chair and crossed over to my desk. Pointing to the shadow questions in the analytic quadrant on the paper, he said, "I know Elena can't stand to see me useless like this. She must be trying to help me by analyzing the situation because all of her questions come from here."

He massaged his jaw for a moment and then went on: "To make matters worse, I've been beating myself up relationally for not looking on the bright side of all of this and instead wallowing in self-pity."

I asked him how he used that kind of inquiry at work when he was helping someone he mentored who was stuck in their thinking. Mark sat back down in the chair and tapped his finger over the relational inquiry quadrant. "Looking at this, I recognize that I have been supportive to the people on my team at work when they're down. I guess I need to give some of what I've been giving to everybody else to myself now. So . . ."

Mark looked up at me, but rather than giving him an answer, I asked him, "How would you be inquiring of yourself if you did that?"

Without pausing, he leaned in and responded, "I guess I'd ask relational questions like, 'How do I really feel about this?' 'What help do I need?' 'Who do I know that can help me get that help?' Then I'd have to listen to whatever answers come, instead of jumping in and telling myself I'm useless."

I let Mark digest what he had just said. When he looked up at me expectantly I pointed to the analytic shadow questions and said, "Mark, this is the kind of inquiry that Elena has been unconsciously using. Since you don't typically inquire analytically, it's a blind spot for you. I imagine analytic questions, *well crafted,* could be of help to you now. Is that true?"

He sat up straight, as if he'd just had an infusion of starch in his backbone, and answered, "You're right about that! Some analysis would come in handy for sure." He tapped the analytic inquiry compass and went on, "She is my little sister after all. There's still a thing or two I can teach her, like how to ask these kinds of questions." He punched my shoulder gently and laughed. "Thanks for the reminder."

How Do You Learn from Your Own Wisdom?

What people think of as the moment of discovery is really the discovery of the question.

—JONAS SALK

Learning your inquiry style helps expand your awareness of what you need. It enables you to find clarity where previously there were blind spots in your thinking and light where there were shadows. There's one last piece of the puzzle that we'd like to offer now, which will deepen and widen the ways you can be in conversation with your own hidden wisdom.

People reach for wisdom because wisdom brings strength.

Without it, your life can feel meaningless and devoid of vitality because you become a bystander rather than a full participant. Learning to find wisdom for navigating the relationships of your life, however, requires a different kind of inquiry, a different way of asking questions that opens you. Think of confusion as the surface turbulence of your mind. Like waves on the ocean, your thoughts can interfere with one another, reinforce one another, or cancel one another out. But if, instead of trying to smooth out the waves, you asked yourself a question such as "What could be beneath this turmoil?" you'd likely dive down and discover the calm expanse of the ocean floor. We call questions that have that effect open questions. They pull you toward the wisdom hidden on the wide-open ocean floor of your mind where you can find meaning and truth and that you didn't even know was there.

Some evocative examples: "What is unfinished for you to give?" "Are you loving the life you are living?" "How are you making your life too small for yourself?" "How can you live divided no more?"

Open questions cause your mind to expand rather than contract; there is no "right" or "wrong" way to answer an open question.

Dawna describes the first time she ever experienced a truly open question:

It was decades ago. I was in a hospital bed, waiting for surgery. I had been told I had terminal cancer. A Jamaican aide who had been mopping the floors sat down in the turquoise plastic chair next to my bed. She breathed with me for a few minutes and then asked, "How can you be more than your pain? How can you be more than your fear?" That's all she ever said to me. After several minutes she got up and disappeared to continue her mopping. My life was never the same. She had offered me questions that I could not answer, but that continue to alter the way I relate to others and myself five decades later.

Any inquiry style can learn from open questions. We have organized some of our favorites in the list below into each of the quadrants. All of them are valuable to consider no matter what inquiry style you prefer. Use them when you are confused, feel disconnected from yourself, or want to expand the possibilities of how you are thinking about an issue.

OPEN QUESTIONS

ANALYTIC

What is right about what seems wrong?
What's the question you don't want to answer?
Why is this *really* important to you?

PROCEDURAL

What did you do in the past to make it through a similar
   challenge?
What is unfinished for you to experience?
What is it too late for? Too soon for? Just the right time
   for?

RELATIONAL

What feeling do you want to have when leaving this
   interaction?
Who causes you to shine?
Who brings out the best in you and how?

INNOVATIVE

What if this situation grew your capacity?
How can you evoke the untamable in yourself, the part
   that dreams and imagines beyond what is known?

What would be happening if you were being advised by
your own future?

PRACTICE: A COMMITTEE OF ONE

*"Clearness Committee" is a simple process for learning that Dawna
was introduced to by the author and educator Parker Palmer. The
Quakers created it in the 1600s as a way to deal with personal
problems in a group. We adopted it because it assumes that everyone has an inner wisdom that can guide them and others. The following solo form is a way of learning that sheds light on cognitive
corners caused by blind spots and shadows. It also helps you learn
how to inquire in all four styles, broadening your capacity to relate
to those who inquire differently. This practice is a gem that will enable you to expand your inquiry repertoire and learn new ways to
access your inner wisdom and resources.*

*Give yourself at least fifteen minutes of uninterrupted time for
this practice. Place the inquiry quadrant illustration at the top of a
piece of blank paper. Imagine that each quadrant represents advisers who are expert in asking analytic, procedural, innovative, and
relational questions.*

*Bring to mind a situation where you feel extremely confused
about relating to another person you care about. Take two minutes
and write a brief summary of your dilemma, being as precise as possible.*

*Next, direct your attention to whatever quadrant is most famil-
iar to you. Write down a few brief questions from that style of inquiry that come to mind. Make sure they are phrased in a genuinely
caring and helpful way rather than disguised advice. For example,
"Have you ever dealt with something like this and not had to struggle?" as opposed to "Could it be that you are having to deal with
issues about your mother?"*

Write a response to the questions you listed.

After responding to the inquiry from your most familiar quadrant, work your way around the other quadrants, writing down questions from each different style, then writing your response. When you've worked your way through each quadrant, stand up and walk for a moment. You have just given yourself a free period of exploration, unencumbered by the limitations of your habitual thinking. In addition, notice any images or insights that may emerge over the next several days.

In the next chapter we will explore how to learn to recognize another's inquiry style and reconcile the differences in the ways the two of you learn.

CHAPTER 7

Reconciling the Differences
in the Ways We Learn

*Every now and then a man's mind is stretched by a
new idea or sensation, and never shrinks back to its
former dimensions.*

—Oliver Wendell Holmes

The ancient sages said that knowing yourself leads to enlightenment; knowing others leads to wisdom. The last chapter offered
you some enlightenment about your own style of inquiry. In this
chapter you'll learn how to discover and reconcile with another
person's style of asking questions so you can learn with each other.
What makes this challenging is that most people know only how
to ask questions of each other that help them "bond." Few know
how to ask questions that bridge the abysses between us.

Bonding happens when two people ask each other questions
until they find a kind of sameness that unites them—family rela-
tions, nations, religions, sports, professions, neighborhood, race,
gender, etc. You learn to do this when you are very young: "Are
you in my family? Do you like X? Do you think Y?" Because of
this, you find out who to turn toward for safety, and who to turn
away from: the "others"—those who are different. The survival of

our species has depended upon bonding. But it can only take us so far. As long as the other person agrees with you, you can stay bonded. If he or she disagrees, however, the only option you have learned is to disconnect or isolate, choose "my way or the highway."

Dawna shares how she learned to bond and how Angie is teaching her the second skill—how to bridge the abyss between them.

My parents were first-generation immigrants. Most of our family was killed by the Cossacks in Russia or by the Nazis in German concentration camps. My mother and father had consequently learned to ask a few questions of someone they had just met and determine whether they were safe or dangerous. They bonded with Jews and became "other-phobic" toward anyone else. Interestingly, all the Jews lived on one side of our street and the Others, the Catholics, literally on the other. No wall between was necessary; they did their own sorting and separating, because differences were not allowed.

I have since learned with Angie that there is a major difference between knowing someone by bonding with them and knowing that person by bridging to him or her. In the first dynamic, you ask questions that probe for ways the two of you are the same. It's so comfortable, so familiar, so confirming. "What's your favorite baseball team? Oh, the Red Sox? So it's you and me against the Yankees and the world, babe!" The two of you agree. Bonding this way is like connecting with duct tape. Though comforting, it seals off anything from the outside, and seals in beliefs, ideas, and positions, which can then be reinforced. You can then blindly continue bound together on the path you are on, not learning as you re-create the mistakes of the past rather than learning a new, permeable way forward.

When I first met Angie almost twenty years ago, I knew immediately that there was little chance of bonding with her in the way I had been taught—not with those high Norwegian cheekbones, long blond hair, and eyes as wide and blue as a summer sky. She was not noisy like the people I grew up with on our side of the street, people who filled every silence within four seconds lest we should all explode into argument or implode into unrelenting grief. Angie naturally speaks softly, asking wide-open questions so both people are on the same side rather than arguing to make a point. This approach was completely foreign to me.

This morning, for example, as we sipped cappuccinos, preparing to write this chapter, my mind began to connect with her by using its own inquiry style. I bubbled out a froth of relational questions: "How did you sleep last night? Can I make you an omelet?" Then I pounced on my innovative agenda before she could get a word in edgewise. "I had a great idea in a dream last night. It will synthesize everything we've already done with this whole new perspective." Remembering that she was my coauthor, I followed up with a question of sorts: "Shall I show it to you?"

Angie smiled at me encouragingly, sipped from her tiny cup, and then opened her computer before saying, "I can hear how excited you are. What's the new idea that's fueling all that passion?"

I proceeded to build a case by wrapping her mind in a magical, mystical story, then a razzle-dazzle plea for how this new way of proceeding could save humanity. Revolutionaries unite!

"I can hear how important this is for you, Dawna. Are you interested in my perspective?" She leaned in, looking straight at me with genuine interest.

My vibes told me she was being sincere. How could I, Relational Mistress of the Universe, not be interested in her perspective? I nodded—reluctantly.

"I love the story you want to add and I'm *also* remembering the goal we set out to accomplish and the structure we created. You said it makes you feel secure and stable."

Angie really seemed to recognize where I was coming from,

but my mind generates new ideas as if they are buttered popcorn in a movie theater, and even though I knew the sequence we had decided on *was* important, it was as hard for me to pull the innovational plug as it would be to sit in the dark and not nibble.

"I love that structure, but let's just try out this one idea I had, okay? Hang in there and you'll see that it will work . . ." I commented.

I'm sure you've heard the expression the "patience of a saint." I think Angie comes by her sainthood by inquiring in such a way that she accepts what I'm saying, without agreeing. We all know how to accept without agreeing. It's like going to see *Star Wars*. You see the Wookiee up there in 3-D on the screen and accept its differences. You don't necessarily have to agree with the Wookiee or even become one. I think of myself as Angie's personal Wookiee. She never expects me to sit down in the theater and become a person like her. She doesn't climb up on the screen to agree with me and become a Wookiee herself. Instead she uses questions to weave an invisible and invincible bridge that connects our different ways of learning what we can make possible together.

But I digress. Back to our writing conversation. "How important is it to you, Dawna, that we write a truly excellent book, one that's clear even to those people who don't learn relationally?" she continued, reminding me of what I had told her only hours before.

What could I say?

"Of course, it's crucially important to me that it's excellent, Angie, especially for people who are very strong rational thinkers but not used to learning relationally."

She nodded and pointed to her computer screen, where yesterday's structure was glowing. "What do you want to do about this, then?" She leaned in, genuinely wanting to know what I was going to say.

I'm pretty good at arguing and convincing. But Angie's questions were evocative instead of provocative. They reminded me of what I truly wanted: for the world to have this book and for all of us to learn how to ask questions that create bridges between our differences. So I took a few breaths, laughed, and proposed a compromise, "All right, dear one, let's look at that structure and *then* envision where we go next."

How Do You Shift from Bonding to Bridging Questions?

Bonding questions search for answers that bring you acceptance and belonging—*as long as you both agree.* "Don't you think that this is a great idea?" Bridging, on the other hand, is about finding the right questions. You inquire to learn how to turn *toward* another who thinks differently until you can find out and accept what is important to them. "What's inspiring you these days?"

This was what Maya Angelou was practicing in such a simple yet profound way as she went through the newspaper. Accepting doesn't necessarily mean agreeing. Accepting means you are momentarily willing to suspend your disbelief. You do this each time you watch a movie. You experience people on the screen who learn differently than you do. You accept them and naturally ask bridging questions inside your own mind to stay connected to them: "What drove that Wookiee to do that?" "What was it like for Luke Skywalker to discover Darth Vader was his father?"

When you are in a conflict with another person in real life it's often difficult to try to put yourself in their position. But what you can do is afford them the same benefit of the doubt, temporarily suspending your disbelief as if you are watching that person up on a movie screen.

Bridging to another person begins with recognizing your own inquiry style, as you did in the last chapter, then discovering the other person's style, and finally bridging to it so you can reconcile the differences in how the two of you learn. In the pages that follow you will find a simple and powerful way to do this.

How Do You Discover Another's Inquiry Style?

Who came to mind as you've been reading about bridging to someone else who inquires differently than you do? In the illustration below we have named the most notable characteristics commonly associated with each inquiry style. Consider what types of questions this person leads with. If you don't immediately recognize the specific style, just be curious about which quadrant(s) their thinking is coming from when they are seeking to learn something.

THE OTHER'S INQUIRY STYLE

Ask for logic behind this. ⑦

Ask for facts and data to explain things. ⑦

Ask questions for clarity. ⑦

Question how to make things efficient and excellent. ⑦

Ask what is wrong, and suggest how it can be fixed. ⑦

Curious about "Why?" in order to pull idea or problem apart for understanding. ⑦

⑦ Ask questions that diverge.

⑦ Ask questions about the future: "What if...?"

⑦ Wonder about alternative scenarios and like to explore options.

⑦ Explore through questions about ideas that help give a new perspective.

⑦ Inquire to create the new, rather than repeating the usual.

⑦ Inquire to synthesize and integrate ideas.

ANALYTIC   **INNOVATIVE**

INQUIRY

PROCEDURAL   **RELATIONAL**

Probe to make sure process is done right. ⑦

Ask about the past and how it is a blueprint for the present and future. ⑦

Ask questions about the outcome, the end result. ⑦

Inquire about best practices, structure, routine, timelines, and rollout. ⑦

Question who is responsible, and own commitments. ⑦

⑦ Curious about how others are feeling.

⑦ Wonder about how things are being communicated.

⑦ Inquire into how to connect different people, ideas, places, things.

⑦ Ask questions that engage and enroll others, developing rapport.

⑦ Ask about how to develop people.

© Angie McArthur

Once you recognize the quadrant from which the other person usually inquires, use the following process to reconcile the different ways you each learn.

1. Know Thyself
   Bring to mind the inquiry style you discovered that you use most often from the previous chapter. This will bring awareness to what kinds of questions are on the tip of your tongue. Angie, for instance, most often asks analytic and procedural questions.

2. Know the Other
   Then listen to the other person, being curious about which quadrant their questions are coming from. In the conversation about writing this chapter, Angie observed Dawna was trying to learn using relational and innovative questions.

3. Bridge to Their Style
   Begin with questions in the style that you believe is most natural for the other person. For example, Angie began with relational and innovative questions in order to bridge to Dawna: "I hear how excited you are. What's the new idea that's fueling all of that passion?" It's helpful to offer an indication that you accept the other's perspective as true for them. Remember, this does not mean you have to agree with them; you merely have to accept it. You don't have to become a Wookiee, but merely be curious about how they perceive the world and what they need. For example, "I get what you just said," or "Now I know how important that is to you."

4. Invite Them into Your Style
   Use inquiry to invite the other person to hear your perspective. For example, "Hearing what's important to you, I'm wondering if you are interested in learning where I'm coming from?" Dawna expresses this with Angie when she

asks: "Are you open to envisioning together where we go next?"

One Plus One Becomes Three

Let's look at this process again in the context of a different kind of dilemma. In the narrative that follows, you'll see Dawna help a couple explore how to come out of the shadows of bonding and use the light of questions to bridge their learning differences.

I had my hand on the doorknob of Jalen's immense home, preparing to leave, when he lobbed a question out of nowhere to me. "Oh, by the way, Dawna, how do you figure out the odds of success for a relationship?" I had spent many weeks working with Jalen—a CEO—and his leadership team, helping them to collaborate more effectively with their customers. As part of that, each of them discovered their inquiry styles. Jalen had been fascinated with identifying and asking questions from different quadrants. Early in his career, he had been a brilliant salesman and he prided himself on being able to pitch to anyone. His secret was that he intuitively "got" anyone, being able to "speak his or her language." The information about inquiry styles just made intuitive sense to him. Now here I was leaving his home at the end of a long working day and he asked perhaps the most revealing question yet, a very important *personal* question when we had almost no time left to explore and address it.

Jalen had totally turned his company around using his relational and analytic inquiry style to champion people and advance the bottom line. He may have been a relational genius in the office, but his "by the way" question indicated that he wasn't equally successful at home. The following week, in their house, he explained further.

Referring to his wife, Lorraine, he said: "I adore her, but

our relationship just isn't working. She tells me I just don't get her, and she sure as hell doesn't get me. Why can't we learn together how to connect with each other anymore? I do what I can to listen and help, but she says I just don't care about what she needs and that makes her feel unsafe with me. I don't know why she says that. It's not logical. I've never hit her or laid a hand on her in anger. I've gone over and over it all in my head. I keep asking her what the problem is, but she keeps freezing me out. Maybe we're just too different. I feel as if I am banging against the door of an igloo." He began to pace back and forth across the white marble floor.

The glass doors opened and Lorraine walked into the room, joining Jalen on the couch. He draped his arm over her shoulder. She immediately got up, moved to the opposite end of the couch, and crossed her long legs at the ankle. She was impeccably sleek from head to toe. Glancing at the Rolex under the cuff of her ivory silk blouse, she looked coolly at Jalen and said curtly, "Well, I'm not late. Why did you start without me?" Before he had a chance to respond, she asked, "Did you offer Dawna something to drink at least . . . or were you too busy telling her what a bitch I am?"

Her questions had been procedural, so I bridged to her mind by asking her to describe a time in the past when she thought that she and Jalen had really been learning together. She told me how, when they had first met, it was like being on an adventure and he seemed to want to listen to her, and learn what she needed.

"Jalen told me you said a great relationship should be like one plus one equals three. Well, we're more like one minus one equals zero. I just don't feel safe with him!"

Knowing that everyone needs different things to feel safe, I asked her to tell me about what had made her feel safe with Jalen when they first met. She responded immediately.

"I feel safe when someone wants to learn how to treat me well, and accepts me for who I am and how I am. Now the

Great Salesman over there seems to care about everyone at work, but all he does at home is try and fix me and all my problems." Lorraine ran her fingers through her short auburn hair. "Someone who loves you doesn't want to fix you. They love you as you are and want to learn how to support you." She wrapped her arms tight around her chest.

Jalen leaned over and asked, "Why won't you be reasonable about this? Why don't you get that I'm only trying to learn how to help you?"

Lorraine snapped back. "I'm not an idiot. I don't need you to fix me or help me. That makes me feel disrespected!"

Jalen looked at me and shrugged. I searched for one small metaphoric question from her world that might begin to bridge this canyon. "Lorraine, you're an antiques dealer. When you're at an auction, what do you call it when people offer a price for something they value?"

Rolling her eyes, she said, "A bid."

"Well, in my business, when one person tries to reach out to another, it's also called a bid, but it's a bid for connection. And usually, after three bids go by without being received, the person offering just gives up trying to learn how to connect."

Lorraine shifted a bit on the couch. "So you're telling me that when Jalen's constantly attempting to fix me he's trying to learn how to connect with me?"

I placed the inquiry styles map on the glass coffee table in front of us and circled Jalen's predominant two quadrants: relational and analytic. I explained that his drilling her with questions about facts and data was a technique that made him a success at work, but was obviously not what she needed to feel that he was on her side. He was inquiring from the shadow side of his analytic quadrant, and he was not using his relational intelligence to learn what she needed. He also wasn't bridging to her way of learning.

She looked at the map and tapped on the procedural quadrant. "So this one is mine? Don't bother to answer that; it's obvious. These are the kinds of questions I always ask: 'How long is it going to take?' 'What's our process?' 'How can we focus this even more?' Inquiring this way is what made me successful." She looked at Jalen and asked, "Given that we learn in such completely different ways, how in the world can we ever reconcile with each other?"

I could almost feel a Möbius strip turning between them. Her question led me to believe that learning was now possible between them. (Refresh your memory about the Möbius strip on page 14.) I reminded myself to bridge to the language of her mental world. I pointed to the shadow procedural questions and asked gently, "Lorraine, when have *you* ever asked these kind of questions? 'Interrogates how things have been done in a critical way, wants to know who's to blame for decisions, asks impatiently about timelines.' And under what circumstances *don't* you?"

She paused, inhaling slowly, and as she released her breath said thoughtfully, "I tend to ask my daughters critical questions about who is responsible for messes around the house, or probe them for exactly how they are supposed to do something or when they have committed to be at home. They call me Nellie the Nag. Elizabeth, our eldest, sometimes calls me Nellie the Nazi, though I don't think she even knows what a Nazi is. I'm puzzled by it because no one at work feels this way. In point of fact, I don't actually ask questions like this at work," she said, tapping a perfectly manicured index finger on the shadow procedural questions.

As she spoke, her shoulders dropped and her neck muscles softened. I decided to probe a little further, sticking as close to procedural questions as I could by asking, "How does it work *for* and *against* you, Lorraine, to ask those kinds of questions?" She stared off into space and tilted her head ever so slightly, before responding, "How it works against me is obvious. Both my daughters no longer want to hang around with me. And I don't like to think of myself as a nag or certainly not a Nazi. I don't really see how it works *for* me . . ." She bit her bottom lip and then continued: "Oh, wait a minute . . . my grandmother raised me. Nanny must have been a procedural learner, too, because she always asked these kinds of questions. When I had the girls, I just figured that all mothers must nag and probe and constantly remind their kids of their responsibilities. So when I do it, I feel like a real mother instead of a fake." Lorraine's eyes welled up with tears, but she immediately grabbed a tissue and blotted them away.

I turned to Jalen, who sat with his arms folded tight. His eyes were also flooded as he sat silently on the other side of the couch. I decided to bridge to him with relational questions in order to help him learn how to connect with Lorraine in some other way besides trying to fix her pain.

"Jalen, my friend, I know you have to make hundreds of decisions on a daily basis concerning the people you lead, right?" He nodded and I went on. "And each of those decisions involves many moment-by-moment choices." I waited for a nod from him before asking, "Have you ever considered that love is a choice also?" Before he could speak, I went on with an open question: "What would happen if, when Lorraine has a problem or issue going on for her, you just asked yourself, How can I choose love right now?"

"I have no idea, Dawna. I realize that my fixing her problems isn't coming across as love. If I asked myself, How can I choose love right now? Well . . . I'd have to let my heart make the decision, not my head."

Lorraine immediately got up, walked over, and sat down at his side. "That's exactly what I want, honey. I do feel safe learning with you when your heart asks questions, but not always with those that come from your CEO head!"

He looked dazed, bemused, totally caught in an unexpected moment. I asked them another open question that I thought would bridge the distance between their differences. "You two have traveled all over the world together, but what if this was a time for the longest journey of all—from your heads to your hearts. Now that your daughters are adults, how can you learn to make choices that grow the love that lives between you?"

I didn't need to wait for an answer.

How Do You Reconcile Your Different Ways of Learning?

Since bridging to someone who learns differently is always a grand experiment, mistakes are not an option—they are a necessity. Lorraine and Jalen illustrate two common errors we all make that keep us from learning with one another: First, without realizing it, they were using different styles of inquiry. Lorraine was attempting to learn procedurally: "What time will we get together?" and her husband was trying to learn analytically: "Why is that important to you?" Neither recognized nor got where the other was coming from.

After recognizing what was happening it was possible for them to learn where the other person was coming from and not take it personally. This enabled them to translate into each other's style of inquiry. Conflicts could now become learning opportunities instead of indications that one or the other was at fault or the relationship was doomed to fail.

The second mistake Lorraine and Jalen made was that they asked each other shadow questions that prevented bridging to each other. She'd frequently asked, "When the hell will things get done around here?" She used a sharp, probing tone of voice asking about timelines. He, on the other hand, had used disingenuous veiled questions like "Don't you get tired of being so uptight?" This resulted in Lorraine feeling unsafe, and Jalen feeling frozen out.

What helped them learn to move beyond this was to take a few breaths, and suspend disbelief in each other as they would in characters on a movie screen. As a result, each began to recognize the shadow questions they were asking.

The illustration below will help you discover some typical shadow questions of each quadrant.

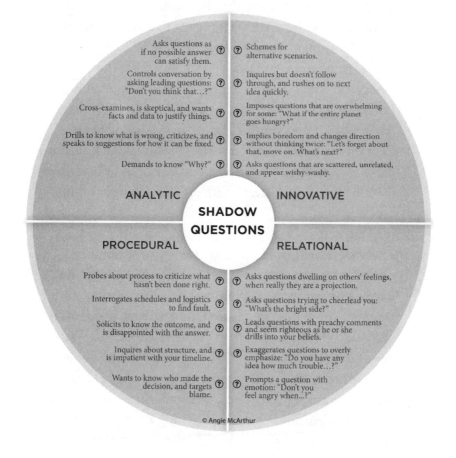

© Angie McArthur

Use it to consider the following:

Know Thyself
> What shadow questions do you tend to ask when you are under stress, scared, angry, or confused?

Know the Other
> What shadow questions are typical of the other person, when they are under stress, angry, scared, or confused?

Bridge to the Other's Style

When you hear shadow questions from the other person
and have identified what inquiry style—analytic, procedural, relational, innovative—is beneath each shadow
question, accept "where they are coming from" and become curious about the need under that question. The
other person may not be using the best wording or gen-
tlest tone of voice, but once you know what they need,
you can create a bridge. For example, when Jalen heard
Lorraine ask, "How long is it going to take?" "What's
our process?" he could recognize her need for procedural inquiry and respond with, "I know these kinds of
practical questions are important to you, so let's address
them first, then I'd like to address some things on my
mind as well."

Invite Them into Your Style

Then it's your turn to translate the shadow questions
you ask yourself and the other person into a constructive conversation. If you know that when you are
stressed, you habitually ask relational shadow questions
such as, "Have you ever stopped long enough to wonder how *I* feel about this?" you can upgrade to authentic relational inquiry. An example would be, "Hearing
that X is important to you, I'm wondering if you are interested in learning where I'm coming from so we can
both walk away having learned more about each
other?"

Using this simple process allows you to create a bridge to another person and turn tense moments into ones of mutual learning.

You now have come to recognize that each of us learns by inquiring in different ways, and that mistakes and failures are just
part of the process. Bridging to another means you are willing to
open your mind beyond confusion, cross over to discover what he

or she needs, and then learn what the two of you can make possible.

In this section you've been discovering how to recognize and reconcile the differences in the ways you and another learn. In the pages that follow, you'll be discovering the mindset that each of you uses to grow so you can increase your capacity to actually create a positive future together.

Discovery Four:

TRUST

Different Ways of Trusting—Through the Discovery of Personal Narratives

CHAPTER 8

Mapping the Way
You Trust

*The mind fits the world and shapes it as a river fits and
shapes its own banks.*

—Annie Dillard

As it flows, the river of your mind shapes itself between the banks
of your basic needs to be safe and to grow. Safety is essential.
Without it, the river floods. Growth is essential. Without it, the
river dries up. If you stay on one side, feeling safe but ignoring
your innate need to grow, you'll find yourself becoming rigid and
stagnant. If you grow but don't feel safe, stable, and secure, you'll
find your life chaotic and frenzied.

Trust is the current of the river that determines how your mind
fits the world. We frequently hear many of the people we work
with say they can't reconcile their differences because the other
person isn't worthy of their trust. We consistently respond with
the question, "What do you need to do or say so you can trust
yourself to be safe and to grow with this person?"

As you've traveled with us thus far, we've been pointing out
how differences in communication, understanding, and learning
appear to be irreconcilable because of an undertow caused by inat-

tention, misunderstanding, and uncertainty. Moving through them depends on knowing how to open your mind to new perspectives.

We also have different ways of growing trust; its undertow is mistrust. Navigating these differences will enable you to move beyond what you previously thought possible. In the previous section you discovered the way you ask questions to navigate differences. In this last section you'll discover how to grow the flow of trust between you and another by navigating the stories you tell yourself.

The Stories We Tell Ourselves

If you could step out of the river of your thoughts and rest on the bank for a few minutes, you would perhaps notice that much of the force that drives the current of your mind is unconscious stories you tell yourself almost continuously. This narrative integrates data and facts from individual moments you've experienced with stories you've been told by family, community, and media. For instance, you might notice the leaves on the tree moving and tell yourself the following horror story: "It's windy. I'd better not sit here too long or I could be blown away, lost and carried by a fierce storm." Or you might tell yourself the following story of possibility: "It's windy! I'll rig a sail and use the wind to help me travel downstream." Your mind is constantly generating stories to either keep you safe or encourage you to grow; whether you trust or mistrust the river, your abilities, your equipment, and the universe itself depends on which of these stories you believe.

The most ignored, mistrusted, and underutilized resource of your relational intelligence is your imagination. It is endowed with spiderlike capacities to weave new stories together from things that your rational intelligence splits into "either/or." For example, when Justin and Alix were divorcing, their lawyers gave them a very rational process for dividing up custody of their children and possessions. That may have been the most effective, rational way to split their assets and childcare, but without a possible relational narrative, the future of their family would have been continually caught in an undertow that pulled everyone to one side or the other. Angie engaged the imagination of both parents and the children in the co-creation of a multidimensional narrative that guided them to find ways to trust each other as they grew a mutually beneficial future. The parents each found one object that represented the vows they had once made but were now changing. Then they found another object that stood for the vows they remained committed to forevermore, including loving and caring for the children. The whole family then made up a "Once upon a time . . ." story that embodied those objects. "Once upon a time two rocks were sitting in a garden. A nest of baby birds was wedged between them. A big wind came along and shook the nest so it fell on the ground. The fledglings were scared at first because it seemed like their whole world had disappeared, but as they explored, they discovered that they could stretch their wings and fly back and forth between the rocks, which were steady and solid and always there for them."

As this story illustrates, your inner mythology directs you to grow apart from or closer to another person. It determines who can be trusted and mistrusted, who gets to be on the "inside" and who the outsiders are. As with any great force of nature, there can be danger and glory in the stories you tell yourself and others. Some of them turn you away from growing trust and some promote it. Some are toxic because they make you feel unsafe and insecure. They keep your problems and wounds festering, and prevent you from letting go of unnecessary habitual limitations. Others are tonic, because they help you define what is needed to grow toward the widest horizon possible.

Recognizing When You Are
Telling Yourself Stories

As you notice the world around you, your brain takes note of data—the specific reality that you see, hear, and feel. Without awareness it quickly metabolizes this data into stories so you can make meaning from what is happening to you. For example, you see a black cat. This is the data. You remember the story that black cats mean danger. You tell yourself that something bad is going to happen to you soon and feel nervous. You experience a churning in your stomach. This becomes your response to seeing a black cat and you may then choose to always run away from black cats! This isn't a rational response to the data—it's an automatic one based on a story you've internalized from an earlier moment.

Until you recognize the stories you are telling yourself, you just assume they are true and believe them. But they have a profound effect on the way you grow because you make unconscious and conscious decisions based on each story.

Many years ago when Dawna was in private practice as a psychotherapist, a Dartmouth College chemistry professor came to see her because he was having serious relational breakdowns with each of the significant women in his life, including the head of his department.

She asked him what he really wanted to learn in their time together. He immediately crossed his arms and told her he couldn't say because he didn't trust her. He explained that he was a rational thinker—a scientist—and she was what he called "a creative" and wouldn't understand him. She responded by asking him for data—the data of his statements about her. It took twenty minutes for him to discover the stories that were determining the future success of their work together. What he shared went something like this: "I see you have red hair and many paintings on the wall. My mother also had red hair and she was an artist. *She* was totally intimidating, never understood me, and I didn't trust her. Therefore, I imagine you are just like her and I'll never be able to trust you, either."

Dawna pointed out gently that he also must be very creative since he had such an active imagination, shaping the future before they'd even had a chance to live fifteen minutes of it. She bridged to him by explaining, in very analytic terms, that the associative wiring in our brains deliberately constructs interpretations of complex and confusing events that are simpler and more coherent than reality. He blushed and they both laughed at the challenge of being such perfectly imperfect humans. The professor had reacted in the same way to the women in his life as you reacted to black cats in the hypothetical story. The work he needed to do with Dawna involved deepening his trust in himself with women by recognizing the limiting stories he was unconsciously creating from the data of his reality. It was those stories that were making him feel unsafe to grow.

PRACTICE: WHAT'S DATA? WHAT'S STORY?

Now it's your turn. Think about how you want to grow trust in yourself.

- Pick one outstanding event that illustrates an area of your life in which you mistrust yourself. For example, work-family balance.
- As you think about that, write down on one side of a piece of paper *just the data* you actually experience. For instance, "When I talk to myself about work-family balance I feel a tightening in my chest, my shoulders droop, and I have an overall sense of being overwhelmed."
- Next, on the other side of the page, note what stories you tell yourself about that data. For example, "I tell myself that work-life balance is impossible. I know I want more time with my family, but the reality is I always have to choose work first. I am just a failure at knowing how to make this happen. But if I don't have more balance I will end up a manic, overstressed person, who snaps at the kids all the time and wears two different shoes to work."
- Consider just the data again. Given what is true, what story could you tell yourself that would enable you to grow trust in yourself? "When I was young, I used to love to roller-skate and had no trouble shifting from one foot to the other. If I stayed too long gliding on one foot, I felt my center of gravity move and I shifted accordingly. I can learn to do the same thing if I think of work as being on one foot and home as the other and check in frequently to make sure I'm gliding back and forth. I think I'll put a little sketch of roller skates on my phone so I remember to shift easily from one to the other."

What *Kind* of Stories Are You Telling Yourself?

Like any great force of nature, the stories you tell yourself hold both danger and glory. There are some that limit your choices and inhibit trust. We call them rut stories. There are some stories that energize your belief in the possibilities available to you and grow trust. We call them river stories. Since they determine the meaning any given person or experience will have for you, it's important to increase your awareness of what kind of stories you are telling yourself and the effect they are having, so you have a choice about the direction in which you are headed.

RUT TO RIVER STORIES

RUT STORIES

Rut Story: A story you tell yourself about the data you observe that limits your choices and prevents growth.

——

Relational intelligence doesn't grow.

RIVER STORIES

River Story: A story about the data you observe that expands your perception and energizes your belief in the possibilities available to you.

——

Relational intelligence will grow.

© Angie McArthur

Rut stories become deeply grooved in your neural pathways. These limiting beliefs flash at hyperspeed, narrowing your perceptions until you see what you have always seen, do what you have always done, and are what you have always been. By telling yourself the same rut story again and again, you continue to reinforce what you cannot do, or cannot be. Your mind clutches them tight, knowing you can count on them because they are familiar. Be it ever so humble, there's nothing as comforting as a rut story.

Rut stories entrance you into believing that the other person has control over you and if it weren't for him or her, you would be free to grow. There *are* times and situations where your growth is controlled by another: if you are a child or in the military, or prison, or an airplane, for example. As you dive into most of your rut stories about whom you can and cannot trust, however, you're apt to discover you inherited them from someone else who was in charge of your well-being or created them when you were a child with less capacity to keep yourself safe.

Alternatively you can tell yourself river stories that expand the possibility of trusting yourself and others. They can lead you to stretch beyond what is known and comfortable. They can urge you to open your hand and reach.

You make up stories about what you hear, what you feel, and what you see all the time without your awareness. Following is an example of how these stories can play out in your mind with even the simplest of visual data: a gray arrow. In the illustration below, the stories in the left column are limiting (rut stories), the ones on the right liberating (river stories). In the first diagram the data is an arrow pointing in several directions. The rut story you might make up is "The arrow is confused and makes me want to lie down for a nap." The river story might be "It's got options to consider!" In the second diagram the data is that the arrow is pointing down in a flaccid way. The rut story you might make up about it is "The arrow is unhappy." Alternatively the river story could be "It must have worked really hard and is justifiably ex-hausted." In the third diagram, the data is an arrow pointed straight ahead. One limiting rut story is "It's pushy." A liberating river story is "It's bold." In the fourth diagram, the data is the arrow that is all squiggly. Your limiting story might be "It's ner-vous to move forward." The liberating story is "It's excited about moving forward."

The following four categories can help you quickly identify the effect of the common rut and river stories you tell yourself and how they inhibit or grow trust in yourself.

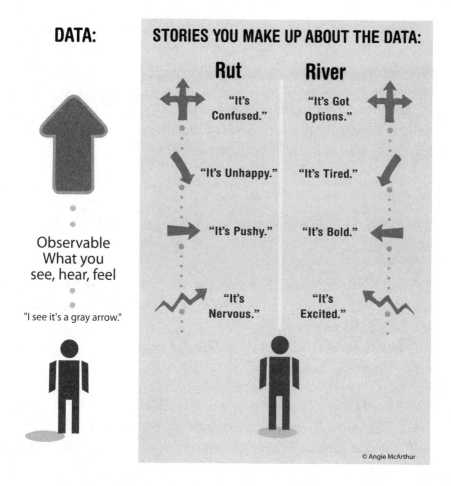

STORIES OF IMPOSSIBILITY/POSSIBILITY

The Data: Your husband is giving you a blank stare.

The Rut Story: You tell yourself he's ignoring you and must be daydreaming about a mistress who is twenty years younger and there is no point in trying to compete with her for his attention. No matter how hard you try, your effort won't make any difference.

   The Effect: You believe you can't get him to relate to you and it's impossible to work through your differences. Just as you don't trust his fidelity, you distrust your ability to influence him.

The River Story: You tell yourself he's thinking deeply about what you have said because he really respects your advice and wants to consider it carefully. Or, "I am continuing to explore ways we can connect and build our understanding of each other."

The Effect: You continue to explore ways you can connect and build understanding of each other's differences. You trust that you can create effective possibilities between you.

STORIES OF INVALIDATION/VALIDATION

The Data: You tell your friend you are hurt because she forgot your birthday.

The Rut Story: As you drive home, you tell yourself you are hyper-sensitive and should have kept your mouth closed because now she'll never forgive you.

The Effect: You mistrust the validity of your feelings, and your need to express them.

The River Story: As you drive home, you tell yourself you are glad you are emotionally mature enough to share what you are feeling and that you need to feel cared about by those who are closest to you.

The Effect: You trust that your feelings are valid and while you know you may be hurt now, you will be able to work through it.

STORIES OF BLAME/CHOICE

The Data: You notice your time sheet indicates that you have worked fifty-six hours this week.

The Rut Story: You tell yourself that your boss will fire you unless you work more than anyone else in the office because he is such a slave driver.

The Effect: You mistrust your ability to set boundaries and blame your boss for not recognizing your needs.

The River Story: You tell yourself that you are very committed to excellence at work and at home. You're a valued employee and it's worth discussing flexible work hours with your boss so you can have more balance in your life.

The Effect: You trust your choices in how to meet your needs for both work and family.

STORIES OF NONACCOUNTABILITY/ACCOUNTABILITY

The Data: During a luncheon with your mother, she lets out a deep sigh and rolls her eyes just as you were explaining why you couldn't come to her fund-raising event.

The Rut Story: You tell yourself your mother makes you crazy because she doesn't understand that you are working full-time, and she always makes you feel bad. Whenever work gets in the way of family plans your mother completely overreacts.

The Effect: You mistrust your ability to communicate effectively the importance of your responsibilities at work *as well as* your caring for her.

The River Story: You tell yourself that it's true your mother is disappointed as a result of your not attending her affair, and you will apologize for the effect that choice had on her. You also realize that you have to make sure you don't disappoint yourself by neglecting what is essential for your own well-being.

The Effect: You trust that you won't disappoint yourself, that you won't neglect what's essential for your own well-being, and you acknowledge that sometimes that may mean disappointing your mother or your boss.

Mapping the Stories You Tell Yourself

Growing trust in how you relate to others requires relating to yourself in a way that makes you feel safe and encourages moving beyond what you thought possible. Mapping the stories you tell yourself will bring fresh clarity about how you are limiting and liberating your capacity. It's important to do this in as nonjudgmental a way as possible. Identifying your stories should never result in you feeling uncomfortable or embarrassed. This is an authentic conversation with yourself that no one else is listening to.

First choose one of the four following domains of your life where you would like to grow trust in yourself: family, work, health, finances. Write down just the data in each one. For example, under finances you may note something like, "I have $30,000 in savings and a steady monthly paycheck of $5,000 a month. My expenses are roughly $4,500 a month." Under family relationships, the data might be: "I have been married for twenty years. I have an elderly father whose needs are increasing. I have two teenage kids who are only at home to sleep and for meals because they participate in sports and other after-school activities."

Next jot down the story you tell yourself about that data and try to identify if it is a river or rut story. Using the same examples as above, under finances you might tell yourself that you've always been able to provide for yourself and family and therefore always will. This would be a river story. Or you might tell yourself that the world is so unstable, you are likely to end up on the streets someday. This would be a rut story.

Under family, you might tell yourself that since you've made it this far, both you and your partner will live happily ever after— a river story—or that 50 percent of all marriages end in failure and since you've been together for twenty years, yours probably will, too—a rut story.

Last, as you review the rut and river stories you are telling yourself, sort out which category (or categories) they fall into: possibility/impossibility; invalidation/validation; blame/choice; nonaccountability/accountability.

In the example we used above, the financial rut stories of ending up on the streets would be narratives of impossibility and nonaccountability, and the one about your marriage ending in divorce would be the same. Mapping these inner narratives makes it easier to reframe the limiting rut stories into ones that help you grow trust in your own ability.

The final step of this process is to reframe your rut stories into river stories. This is the way to create a more positive future.

What follows are some examples of how people we have worked with have done this in various domains.

REFRAMING IMPOSSIBILITY/POSSIBILITY

The Rut Story: A successful relationship shouldn't require effort. "If I need to work so hard at this, there is something wrong with the relationship and it obviously wasn't meant to be."

The River Story: A breakdown is a chance to help each of us learn something about ourself and the other. "What do I need to learn so I trust myself and the other person to create a possible future?"

REFRAMING INVALIDATION/VALIDATION

The Rut Story: The other person should know what I want and need if they care about me. "I'm not giving you the satisfaction of telling you what I want, because you should know by now."

The River Story: Since we can't read each other's mind, I'll be growing my understanding of what the other person needs for the rest of my life. "I don't understand what you need right now, so teach me how to treat you well."

REFRAMING BLAME/CHOICE

The Rut Story: My personality is my personality. I've always been this way. Problems mean you or I have some kind of flaw. "It's my way or the highway. If you disagree with me, you are just wrong."

The River Story: I change as I grow and learn. "I know that we're having a problem right now and I trust that we'll find a way to learn through it."

REFRAMING NONACCOUNTABILITY/ACCOUNTABILITY

The Rut Story: Disagreement means we can no longer be close. "If we don't agree, there is just no point in continuing any further."

The River Story: Disagreement can widen my horizons by giving me a new perspective. "I may not agree, but I accept that what you are saying is important for you."

How Do You Transform the Stories You Are Telling Yourself?

There are some domains of your life where you are less likely to feel safe because you are telling yourself rut stories and other areas where you tell yourself river stories and therefore trust your capacity to grow. Review a rut story you know you tell yourself in any domain of your life and consider how you can transform it *without anyone else having to change at all*. For example, you could ask yourself, What needs to change in the way I am relating to her so that I feel safe enough to trust myself no matter what she does?

In the following story, Angie shares how she helped a doctor transform a limiting story to one of possibility.

I sat across from a fifty-nine-year-old French cardiologist, J.D. His home office had bookshelves filled with hundreds of worn encyclopedias, medical journals, travel guides, histories, and spy novels. Interspersed between them were photos of family members, Japanese kimonos, Thai elephants, grinning Australian bushmen, and Malaysian woodcarvings. As I took it all in, my mind wandered to each of these distant places. I was struck by the breadth of experience this man had. I shook myself back to the present moment, refocused, and asked J.D. what was going on for him. His voice cracked. "I think I have failed to provide enough money for my family's future," he said wistfully.

I knew J.D. and his wife, Carol, had been hoping to retire the following year and the financials were daunting. He came from a generation where a man's worth was based on the security he provided for his family. But retirement had always seemed like a far-off concept to both of them. They hadn't even considered saving for it until they were both in their fifties. A financial planner they recently consulted commented that they had spent more time preparing for exotic vacations than for their retirement.

J.D's head dropped as he recited the long list of dismal rut stories he was imagining: "Well, I suppose we can live on half of what we do now if we don't travel to see the grandkids . . . if we don't get injured, or ill . . . and if we eliminate spending on anything that isn't absolutely necessary . . ."

With each "if" his neck muscles tightened until they were like steel cables. Leaning his chin against the palm of his hand, he continued, "Well, it means we can't live like the Campbells and go to Arizona in the winter. And we can't live like the Singhs and take the grandkids to Hawaii. And of course we won't live like the Ashtons and build our dream house . . ." It was clear to me that he was handicapping himself with rut stories about what he imagined retirement would be. In his diagnosis of the future, they would be living less in every way.

I interrupted him. "Does the way these friends live inspire you?"

He shook his head. "No, not really. I mean they have security . . . play a lot of golf, fish, they do what they want, but those aren't the things I'm inspired to do."

I put my hand on his shoulder and asked, "J.D, who do you know who's retired and living in a way that does inspire you?" He placed his elbow on his knee and cupped his jaw.

"There's this one doctor friend of mine who lives in the UK. He's remained sharp, sends very clever emails about fascinating online university courses he's taking like 'Modern Ethics,' 'WWII and Society,' 'The Future of Big Data.' He's still learning and he's still giving. He was a pediatrician and now volunteers once a year for a stint in Africa. He gets to spend a lot of time taking his grandkids to soccer matches, and is teaching them chess."

I then asked J.D. to consider the domain(s) of his life where he was excited about the future. He didn't need time to think before blurting out, "This great charity organization I am a part of that is raising money to care for the elderly in need . . . And also the men's choir I sing in every week."

I asked him what stories he was telling himself about these two. It took him a minute to consider the question, but then he beamed—"I just love the charity organization, and helping those who are even older than I am. It makes me feel young. They laugh at my bad jokes. I can imagine myself being of service to them for a long time. As for the men's choir, I am already imagining the performance we'll do next year at the holidays. I love thinking of all my grandkids hearing that old men can still sing. I know I can only get better and better with age." I shared how these river stories of his friend, the charity, and his singing could help him rewrite his internal limiting narrative about retirement.

I bent toward him and asked curiously, "J.D., let's go back to your friend. What do you admire in him that you most want to grow in yourself?" He looked at me, winked, and replied, "I see where you're going with this—obviously I'd admire the ways he keeps on learning and giving." Smiling back, I replied, "Good. So what kind of future can you imagine for yourself that grows *your* capacity to do this?" His face lit up, as he said, "Not much different than what I described for my friend. I'd love to take classes so I can continue to learn. I could take temporary positions for doctors on leave and practice medicine for short stints in interesting places. That would allow us to travel a bit as well as bring in some additional income. I'd like to take long walks with Carol, go to the movies, and maybe teach my grandkids about music. They both seem to love to sing, like I do."

"So let me do a reality check. Is that a future you can imagine providing for yourself and your wife?"

He ran his fingers through his curly black hair and then threw his shoulders back so his chest expanded as his vision did the same.

I probed a little deeper, asking, "Earlier, when you said you had failed to provide for the future, who were you thinking you'd failed?"

He took a slow breath as he considered the question. Then he replied, "I sincerely don't know now. I guess going through all this retirement planning stuff, I got really caught up in the brochure images that Carol showed me of what retirement is supposed to look like; I knew I couldn't have the Arizona house, golf membership, and palm trees, but—"

I put my hand up to stop him and asked, "You can't have, or don't really want to have?"

Laughing he nodded his head. "You're right. Being a doctor, I guess my biggest fear is losing my mental faculties. I really don't know who I'd be if I wasn't somehow learning, treating, and giving to people."

I reached over for his stethoscope and said, "Even if you do lose your mind, it's obvious you're not going to lose your heart as long as it's included in your plans."

The thing many people are actually the most afraid of is their own rut stories. You need to know you can keep yourself safe in order to grow. Rut stories can cause you to mistrust your own capacity to do this. Imagine paddling down a rapid river while constantly reminding yourself of all the dangers that could be lurking around the next bend, and how easily you could drown, and how your paddle could break in two and how the universe isn't really a friendly place and . . . These stories would cause you to mistrust the river, your abilities, your equipment, and the universe itself.

It is true that all life is impermanent and each of us is responsible to do whatever she can to maximize safety, based on the data of the real threats that life brings. It is also true that it's more effective to notice those threats and protect yourself from them without the distortions that your imagination can create in the form of rut stories.

Elizabeth, for example, grew up with a father who was a successful athlete and entrepreneur, but her mother, an alcoholic, had gone from one failing relationship to another. Elizabeth grew up hearing only rut stories about how love relationships stifle a woman's choices and she drank these in with her mother's milk. In business and sports, she trusted her capacity to risk growth and embraced it without hesitation. But with friends and lovers, she kept capsizing in the flood of rut stories that filled her mind as soon as she began to grow close to anyone. Over and over, as soon as she dove a little deeper with someone, they would "betray" her in some way and she would swim away as fast as she could. She finally came up for air when Dawna asked her what she needed to do or say to trust herself with someone she was close to. Elizabeth realized that she could give others boundaries. She could teach them how to treat her well, something that would have been impossible with her alcoholic mother. This enabled her to create river stories and grow toward the greater intimacy that was her birthright.

In the next chapter you'll discover how to recognize another's stories and reconcile the differences in how each of you grow trust.

CHAPTER 9

Reconciling the Differences in the Ways We Grow Trust

Since we cannot readily reshape our partners to match our fantasies, we may have to reshape our fantasies to match our partners.

—Frank Pittman

You know what growing apart from someone feels like. Chances are you've had the experience many times and surely you've heard stories of it from friends or seen it depicted on television. It's often talked about with an accompanying shrug, as in, "What can you expect? Over time people just grow apart."

But growing *together* is a less obvious and even an unexpected process. Sometimes it's ascribed to luck or "falling," as in falling in love. Does it just happen by chance with the right person? How do you "do" it?

Growing together is an art form that requires trusting in yourself *with* the other person as you venture into the unknown. As such, it compels you to use the deepest and widest power of your mind—imagination.

Imagination creates the current of trust or undertow of distrust between you and another. What do you do when someone is mistrusting you? How do you regain the buoyancy of trust after you've lost it? How do you shift the limiting stories you are telling yourself about another person to ones that liberate your natural capacity to grow together? Angie shares how she learned to grow together with Dawna by reclaiming her trust in herself.

My unspoken words to Dawna were choking me. I couldn't get the feelings I was experiencing to form into cohesive thoughts, let alone words. Whatever rose in my mind, I negated. I would be stuck sitting next to her for five more hours as we flew from Amsterdam to New York. The aircraft was oversold, and over-stuffed with coughing people, some wearing masks due to the latest outbreak of SARS. Dawna leaned over toward me: "That was great work, Angie. I am so thrilled. John said it was trans-formational for him and his team. As CEO, he put himself on the line to bring us in, and he couldn't ask for a better result. Yay!" She lifted her hand to high-five me, but I only halfheart-edly raised mine. I wanted to join in the celebration but I was brooding, still trying to form the words I really wanted to say. The fact that she had a totally different experience of the event than I did agitated me even further.

I was in my early thirties and had been told by many people I was "difficult to read." It had always seemed easier to battle my negative thoughts on my own rather than bare them to the world; I assumed they had no value. I squirmed as my shoulder touched Dawna's. She turned to me and in a soft voice asked, "Is there something I'm missing—do you not think it went well?"

My discomfort grew and it wasn't only because I was sit-ting in the middle seat. "No, it was great. You did a superb job. I just . . . but I couldn't . . . You didn't . . . You must think . . . I wasn't . . ." Trying to explain only produced unintelligible word salad. She turned back to face the front of the plane, her eyes lowered.

I just gave up trying to talk. Stuck between not wanting to

complain and not believing my own feelings had value, I crossed my arms, and resolved it was best for me to just suck up feeling mistrusted. I didn't know a way out. I turned my head toward her and took one of my favorite verbal escape routes: I apologized. "I'm sorry, I'm not currently in the right headspace for any constructive conversation. Let's pick this up later, okay?" My discomfort grew.

Dawna took a couple of deep, slow breaths and took out her computer and favorite flight magazines. She adjusted the headrest, placed the blanket over her legs, and pressed a pillow behind her lower back, making herself as comfortable as possible.

Just as she was about to open her laptop she turned and asked if she could "check out" with me a story she was telling herself.

"Sure," I said, thinking she had meant to say, "Could I *share* a story with you." Any diversion was welcome.

"I notice your shoulders are pulled in and tense, Angie. I realize you're in a middle seat and we have a long flight ahead, yet the story I am telling myself is that you are unhappy with the workshop or something I did. Is that true?" Bam, she had read me cold; I felt exposed. I heard her words right in the center of my chest.

"Well, I did think the work was great, but I . . ." I didn't want to complain.

"Angie, please give me the chance to learn to grow with you. You know how much I love to learn. I have no idea what I did that upset you. We can't learn to trust each other if you won't teach me how to treat you well." I was bemused, unsure how to proceed. I never had someone ask me how they could learn to treat me well.

"Go back to the moment you felt mistrusted, and just describe what you actually experienced. Then share with me what story you imagined from that data." As she described this process my shoulders relaxed and I could feel my throat begin to loosen. Because she asked me, I felt safe enough to share what I had been thinking.

"When we designed the agenda a month ago, we decided that after the first ten minutes, I was going to facilitate a piece on framing questions. I spent literally hours preparing. When that time came for me to speak, you were in the midst of a story, and you just rolled right into other content and then questions from the participants. You completely forgot my piece. Then a participant asked for my name and wanted to know who I was. So, the data is you forgot to introduce me and let me facilitate my piece. What I imagined was that you don't trust my contribution—meaning me."

Her eyes wide, Dawna leaned toward me and exhaled slowly before she asked, "Angie, do you want to ask me if what you imagined was true?" I nodded, and haltingly looked at her as I said, "Is it true? Do you not trust me?"

She rested her hands on her computer and lowered her eyes for a moment before telling me that it was true she had forgotten to introduce me and the piece I was going to deliver. Then turning toward me, she looked right into my eyes and said, "It's not true that I don't trust the contribution you make or you!" She went on to give me very specific examples of what I did to support the program being a success. I could tell she wasn't just saying these things to pamper my bruised self-worth. It was obvious that she was, in fact, offering *her* perspective of the same event.

My chest opened, and I began to take deeper breaths. Dawna said, "Angie, the stories you carry inside your mind can either soften or harden your heart." She placed her palm on top of mine and continued: "It hurts me to know you've been carrying around that rut story since yesterday. We have limited time together, Ange. I'll make a thousand mistakes with you, but you have to know that I really want to learn how to treat you well, and I can only do that if you risk telling me the stories you are imagining and then check them out with me. It's the only way we can really grow: by learning how to trust ourselves with each other."

Dawna gave me an invaluable gift that day: the process of checking out my stories. I now call it "reality check." It has become my favorite way to work through messy mishaps and misinterpretations with people I care about. If I feel mistrust, I jump right in unabashedly, state the data and what I imagine. Finally the part that's still a little nerve-racking: I check out whether my story is true. It's the cleanest, most genuine way to reconcile our differences. And as Dawna would say, "We have so little time. Why waste it?"

After fifteen years of practicing reality checks I've found that they are equally useful if the other person confirms your worst imaginings. It can be a huge relief to know what stories you are actually dealing with. This clarity brings you closer to creating mutual trust.

You may also find, as I did, that using this process makes it possible for you to shift from limiting to liberating stories. Before this interaction with Dawna I told myself a rut story that others wouldn't trust the value I could bring. When I came up against an obstacle with someone, I told myself stories that reinforced it wasn't worth trying to explain myself.

In learning to do reality checks with those closest to me, my mindset has shifted; I now tell myself a river story about how obstacles are an opportunity to grow closer to others and myself.

How Do You Shift from Growing Apart to Growing Trust?

Two people can see/hear/feel the same thing and then create two completely different stories about its meaning. When you can understand the stories formed in the other person's mind from the original data it's easier to reconcile differences. Who came to your mind as you read Angie's story about how she learned to grow beyond mistrust? Who is there in your life that you tell yourself rut stories about? Who do you think tells themselves rut stories about you? How would it benefit you if you could move beyond these differences? Would you, for instance, free up mental energy, feel more possibility about the future, and deepen your trust in yourself?

Be brave. Allow yourself to do a reality check with the person you were just thinking about, as outlined below. It will take you from the specific data of reality to naming what you imagined and finally to checking out if what you imagined is indeed true for the other person. If that feels too risky, pick someone at first with whom you feel more comfortable experimenting with new behavior. The steps are:

1. Tell the other person you have something you want to check out with them and ask if they are willing to do it with you.
2. **Check** the **data** by naming it.
3. **Check** the **story** you imagined from the data with the other person.
4. **Check** out the **truth** of that imagined story with the other person.

Dawna describes how a couple she worked with learned to use the reality check to reconcile their differences and grow together.

GROWING BEYOND MISTRUST

"I've spent my entire life loving to learn. Now it's time for me to learn how to love . . . a man." Ramona was a fifty-something professor of Asian American studies at a prestigious East Coast university. As she sat on the tan leather couch in my office, I thought of a swan that appeared to be gliding smoothly across a pond but was, in fact, paddling furiously beneath the surface to stay afloat. Marcus, her fiancé, was exactly the opposite. He was short, compact, solid as a redwood, but his mind moved as fluidly as the wind. He had used his analytic brilliance to become the first African American CFO of one of the largest banking firms in the world.

I asked them to tell me how I could support the way they were relating to each other. Ramona stood up and circled the room, gesturing emphatically as she spoke. "I know we are in love with each other; that's never been in question. Sometimes, though, I have big doubts as to whether we should be getting married. I keep bumping into all of our differences. He's a methodical planner who loves to watch football games on TV. I'm creative, wild, a perpetual learner who is used to having my own way. Even though I love to learn, I'm seriously doubting whether I can learn anything with and from him because, well . . . I just don't trust him right now." Ramona paused and then said, "That's how you can help me. Help me understand how I can trust Marcus, and more important, how can I trust myself *with* him? This whole growing a future together feels impossible and overwhelming."

Marcus rubbed his forehead, leaned forward, and locked eyes with me. "One thing she didn't mention is that she was in three previous long-term relationships with women. She'd never been with a man before we fell in love. In fact, I am the first man she's dated since college. On my side of our divide is the fact that all of the women I've been with lived in foreign countries. I've always had a 'back door' so I could escape when things got intense by returning home to the States." He turned and looked steadily at Ramona. "But I know *she's* the one. I don't want to get away from Ramona." He exhaled and patted the couch. When she slid down beside him, I could feel the spark between them even though I sat on the other side of the room.

"Dawna, you asked how you can support us growing a future together. Damned if I know." Marcus looked at me steadily, then continued: "And that's the problem. Neither one of us grew up with parents who were together or even a father who was around, for that matter. None of my current friends are in monogamous relationships and Ramona's friends are all lesbians. I hear her say she wants to stick around and learn how to trust a man who sticks around. Well, I need to learn how to *be* trusted as a man who sticks around."

My mind began flashing ideas and questions like a lightning storm, but I decided to let their stories settle. Ramona was the first to speak. "There's a lot of things we do really well together, but we don't know how to fight well. We keep slipping into a blame-shame game. I had enough of that growing up."

"For instance?" I asked.

"Last month, for instance. Marcus took off on a business trip to Spain. When he returned, I asked him why he hadn't invited me to go with him. All he said was that business is business. Then he changed the subject. I asked again. This made him furious. He shut down tighter than a clam and turned on a Dallas Cowboys game. (He knows I'm a Giants fan!) I was ripshit. I knew where this was going to go, so I stomped out of the house and slept at my friend Susannah's apartment."

The muscles under Marcus's jaws tightened. He leaned forward and bit off each word that came out of his mouth. "You don't trust me at all, do you?"

I held up my hand and exhaled very slowly, loud enough so that both of them could hear. Then I explained that the more aware they could each be of their internal physical experience, the more able they would be to observe their thinking and grow trust in the moment. I asked them to notice the sensations in their bodies and the rhythm of their breathing.

After a few moments we each seemed to settle in and settle down. I turned toward Ramona and asked, "You're a passionate and imaginative woman. I also know that you're enough of an academic to respect data and reality. Is that true?" She nodded. "I'd like to introduce you to an alternative to the blame-

and-shame game which, as you demonstrated, just leads to fight and flight. You could call it the reality check. It helps you sort out fact from fancy, so you can shift to the kind of mindset that will help the two of you reconcile your differences and grow trust between you. Are you willing to learn something new?" Ramona nodded, looking both sheepish and intrigued.

"Okay. This game requires that you check out what you are imagining to find out if it's true for Marcus. If it's not, then it must be true for *you* somehow." Both of them were staring eagerly at me so I continued: "Ramona, step one requires that you separate out the data of what happened from the story that you imagined. It's like sorting out the different colors and the delicates in laundry. Begin by naming one fact that you actually experienced that afternoon. Then tell the story your very fertile mind made up from that fact. Finally, check it out by asking Marcus if it's true for him. If he says no, we can check it out to see if it's true for *you*."

Her spine elongated as she folded her long arms across her chest and asked, "But what if he lies to me about it being true?"

I looked directly into her hazel eyes and replied, "He may, in fact, not tell you the truth, but you can *guarantee* that he won't if you blame and shame him. Also, it may be something you project onto him because of your past or because you don't want to own it. You can't do it wrong. We'll go step-by-step and I'll help you through the process."

She unfolded her arms and took three breaths. "Okay. I'll give it a try: Marcus, you went on a business trip. I imagined you had a wild fling with someone you met there." She was about to go on, but I interrupted by putting my hand softly on her knee, to remind her that she had to pause and check out with Marcus if that was true.

He turned so he could look directly at her. Then he quietly said, "No, baby, that's not true."

Ramona turned to face him directly and went on, "Okay, but when I asked why you didn't take me, did you just change the subject? No, wait, don't answer that. I have to do the reality check thing. I noticed you didn't answer my question the second time I asked it and instead turned on the Dallas game. I *imagined* you were really pissed because I caught you cheating, so you wanted to shut me out. Is that true?" Her eyes were flashing.

Marcus looked away briefly, then turned back and responded, "I was pissed, but not for the reason you thought. I've worked really hard to do what I've never done and stay loyal to you on that trip. That didn't matter at all; you were blaming me anyway, and I feel really mistrusted."

Ramona blinked several times, and then added, "What about the Cowboys game? I saw you turn that on, and . . ." She glanced at me and then continued: "I imagined you were trying to get me pissed. Is *that* true?"

Marcus reached over and took her hand in his, saying, "Guilty as charged, my darling."

None of us could resist laughing. He glanced over at me and said, "Is it my turn yet?"

I nodded and without letting go of her hand, he looked at Ramona and asked, "Baby, I saw you walk out the door. I heard the next day that you went to Susannah's house, and, well, I did some imagining of my own. I imagined *you* were tempted to have a wild fling just to get back at me." He looked over at me before adding, "Is that true?"

Ramona looked up at me, took a deep breath, and then replied, "I cannot tell a lie. The thought did cross my mind, but then, just like one of your Cowboys, it kept on running. Old habits die hard, but they do, they *will*, die." Marcus threw his head back and laughed. Then he said, "This reality check stuff is scary as shit but I think that learning to really trust ourselves *with* each other so we can grow closer is worth it." He stood up, pulled Ramona into his arms, and winked at me. "Touchdown!"

How Do You Reconcile Different Ways of Growing Trust?

Marcus's and Ramona's initial blame-and-shame rut stories were based on their previous histories, which were minefields that had the potential to blow up their future together. Using the reality check process gave them a new approach to trusting themselves with each other. How can it help you do this?

Think of your imagination as a movie projector. Think of the person you are relating to as the big white screen in front of the theater. Your imagination finds some aspect of yourself that you don't trust, that you are embarrassed by or ashamed of, and disowns it. For example, you might think of yourself as a loving person and therefore disown your occasional fits of anger. Without being aware of doing so, you project this aspect as a movie onto the screen. "*He's* such an angry person." Ramona did this unknowingly when she projected the part of herself that wanted to have wild flings onto Marcus and imagined he was cheating. He, on the other hand, had projected his anger onto her and imagined that she didn't believe him.

When Dawna asked Ramona to take another step in the reality check by owning the wild part of herself instead of projecting it onto Marcus, it gave both of them a blank screen on which they could grow enough trust to move forward.

You may be thinking, But what if he *had* told her that he did have a fling? Or, what if he had an affair and lied about it? In either case, regardless of what Marcus said or did, Ramona trusted her ability to face reality and learn from it, rather than escalate it by having an affair just to get even with Marcus. In order to grow trust with another person you need to reclaim the positive and negative aspects of yourself you project onto another. Once you have brought them home you can find out what they really need so you can trust yourself.

Growing Trust by Reclaiming
Your Projections

You can reclaim both negative and positive projections by adding the last step to the reality check process:

1. Check the **data.**
2. Check the **story** you imagined from the data with the other person.
3. Check out the **truth** of that imagined story with the other person.
4. Check the **projection** by asking yourself, Is what I imagined about the other person ever true for me?

Remember, we coauthor our future with the stories we tell each other and ourselves. You have been learning to grow trust by navigating the journey from rut to river. Every reach across an old limiting barrier of mistrust liberates a possible future. In the last chapter we offer you one practice and one story to support growing from each other.

CHAPTER 10

Growing from Each Other

By love I mean that condition in the human spirit so profound it encourages us to develop courage and build bridges, and then to trust those bridges and cross the bridges in attempts to reach other human beings.

—Maya Angelou

We began this book with a story about the relational genius Maya Angelou, and a practice she used to grow by finding the best and worst of others in herself. In chapter 1, we also shared how the two of us began our journey together, stumbling over, struggling through, and striving past our differences until we could find respect for them. The word "respect" means "to see again as if for the first time." The greatest gift we can give each other and ourselves is willingness to question our biases, see past our blind spots, and discover each other again.

In the previous chapter you discovered how you sometimes unknowingly project negative aspects of yourself onto others. Now we offer a way to discover how you can use projection to grow yourself. The practice will help you see positive aspects of yourself that you may have ignored as if for the first time. The two of us used it on the day we finished this manuscript. We began in solitude by each of us writing a brief letter describing what it was we most respected about the other person. We then sat across from each other reading aloud:

Dear Dawna,

I respect the way you are always willing to dive into murky challenges undaunted.

I feel less lost when you share with me what is important to you. Your willingness to try new things and constantly seek excellence encourages me to dive deeper than I thought possible. I am inspired by your ability to stick with unanswered questions until the ripples of their learning have touched you. I trust your capacity to hold truth, no matter how difficult. I admire your genuine desire to support others finding and nurturing their uniqueness. Writing this book with you has been a privilege, a dream realized, and a teaching.

Love, Your Co-Authorette

Dear Ange,

What I most respect about you is the way that, no matter what, you dig in with me. No matter how obstinate or divergent or stubborn I can be, you sit quietly next to me, waiting for the chance to ask a great question. You refuse to be intimidated and you also refuse to intimidate. Fear just doesn't want to grow anywhere near you. I also respect your undaunted willingness to be a beginner who persistently cultivates her own wisdom. Though you were born from Norwegian stock, you sure do have a lot of chutzpah! I'm so grateful you would not let me give up on writing this book the 10,000 times I wanted to just "take it easy." You always encouraged me to take the higher ground.

Mahalo Nui Loa, Authorette D

Next came the awkward part. Next came the projection part. Next came the important part. We each went to a different room, stood in front of a mirror hanging on the wall, and read back the letter we wrote to the other person, *substituting our own name,* as if the letter were written to ourselves instead of the other. Angie looked in the mirror and read to herself, "Dear Angie, I respect the way *you* are always willing to dive into murky challenges undaunted. I feel less lost when you share with me what is important to you."

Dawna looked into the mirror and read the letter she wrote to Angie for herself: "Dear Dawna, What I most respect about you is the way that, no matter what, you dig in with me. No matter how obstinate or divergent or stubborn I can be, you sit quietly next to me, waiting for the chance to ask a great question."

We invite you to use this letter-writing practice with one other person with whom you thought you had irreconcilable differences. You may be tempted to skip over it rather than ask someone else to do it with you, but we strongly encourage you to do it anyway. If you don't want to ask the person to do it, write the letter to them anyway and read it back to yourself in the mirror. It may at first seem "vain," but the effect is actually the opposite.

You will discover the hidden roots beneath the surface that are nurturing and sustaining you; you will discover that the other person (your letter recipient) has been helping you grow all along. The respect that is generated by this practice is for the other person, for yourself, and especially for the intelligence, the hidden root system between you.

Curses to Blessings

We all grow from one another, rooted in the blessings, dreams, and wisdom of those who came before us as well as supported by those who stand next to us. This last story originated from Dawna's grandmother. We've shared it with people we work with, and now offer it to you.

We were working with Charlie and Emily at a retreat we were facilitating at the Sundance Resort in Utah. They communicated differently, learned differently, understood differently, and grew trust differently. Charlie, the president of the company, was a master worrier as well as an inspirational corporate warrior. Emily worked closely with him as head of marketing. She was relatively young and new in her job but had climbed the ladder of success with great energy and foresight. Because of the stress of a financial downturn, Charlie had been trying to help Emily grow by telling her what he thought she should do, given his experience in the corporate culture. For her part, Emily was worried that Charlie wasn't nimble enough to change with the times. Their best efforts to help the other grow had fragmented and disintegrated into backstabbing and a complete breakdown of their ability to relate effectively to each other.

We began by asking each of them to think of someone in their life whose differences had been really annoying. We asked Charlie to share a story of a time he had secretly cursed the future of that person without telling us who he was thinking about. Charlie sheepishly replied, "Hey, you SOB, I hope someday you choke on your own loud and obnoxious words!" We laughed and turned to Emily and asked her to do the same. Grinning, she followed quickly: "I hope that the IRS auditor checks on her own spreadsheets." Then Charlie began to look around the room and put his arms across his chest. He clearly was uncomfortable with where he thought this was going.

Angie went on anyway. "Obviously, you are both experts in knowing how to use your imagination to curse the future of another person. I'd like to ask you something. What effect do you think it has on a partnership, friendship, or relationship when the people involved in it are secretly cursing each other's future?"

Charlie uncrossed his arms and said, "Well, obviously, it tears the partnership apart. The respect disappears and they both lose. I never thought about it this way before but the same thing must naturally happen with a couple or a friendship."

Dawna nodded and explained that her grandmother had told her that blessings were the hidden side of curses. Both Charlie and Emily sat completely still. She went on, "You're obviously both proficient cursers. Do you also know how to transform those curses into simple blessings?" For instance, the curse of that SOB would become a blessing that in the future he learns to skillfully express his frustrations. Or that the woman learns in the future how she can compassionately deal with others' financial frailties.

It was Emily who looked uncomfortable now, but Dawna invited them both to look at the center of each other's chest. She asked that they imagine vividly that the other was using his or her difficult differences as resources to create a possible future. They both looked confused, but then the room dropped into a very luscious stillness. Shortly thereafter, we heard Charlie say, "I could bless a future where you are surrounded by skillful and articulate people. May it be so!" Emily's eyes filled with tears as she whispered, "I bless a future where you continue to inspire others with grace and ease. May it be so!"

Angie asked both of them to notice what it felt like to be in a room where someone who had previously been irritated by their differences was now blessing their future. The energy rose like Dawna's grandmother's bread dough. She asked of them each to name someone they cared very much about who was *not* in the room, someone who they wanted to experience what it felt like to have their future blessed in this way. Charlie called out his son's name; Emily, her sister's. Without instructions to do so, the three of us all said in unison, "May it be so."

As you read these words, please know that you have been *our* blessing because you have inspired this book through us. Please know that in this moment we are blessing your future.

We offer the following questions in gratitude to those who came before you, those who stand next to you, and those who will follow you:

What if you think relationally as well as rationally?

What if you inspire others with stories that enrich life to balance those that diminish it?

What if you dignify differences in communication, understanding, learning, and growing trust to cultivate relational intelligence between you and those who matter?

May it be so!

PANDO

The largest living species on the planet is an aspen grove in Utah. Scientists have named it Pando, Latin for "I spread." It has an intertwined root system beneath the surface that stretches hundreds of miles. This allows trees, which stand in dryer areas, to receive water and nutrients, ferried by roots standing in wetter soil. One tree supports another. These aspens know how to thrive in instability. The potentially devastating events of fire, avalanche, and mudslides actually encourage the aspen root system to react by sprouting more growth.

CARDINAL RULES OF RECONCILING DIFFERENCES

1. You can't change the other person—even for his or her own good. You can, however, grow your capacity to relate to them, to dig in with them.
2. You can't make them love, respect, or even like you, unconditionally or any other way. You can, however, find a

way to respect yourself and how you are relating to the other, no matter what.

3. You can't prove to the other person that your perspective, needs, and way of doing things are right, or better than his or hers. You can, however, grow your ability to recognize, accept, and value each of your differences.

APPENDIX

VKA⇔AKV

Visual, Kinesthetic, and Auditory VKA PATTERN				Auditory, Kinesthetic, and Visual AKV PATTERN			
V1		FOCUSED THINKING	To Trigger Concentration: VISUAL	A1		FOCUSED THINKING	To Trigger Concentration: AUDITORY
K2		SORTING THINKING	To Trigger Sorting: KINESTHETIC	K2		SORTING THINKING	To Trigger Sorting: KINESTHETIC
A3		OPEN THINKING	To Trigger Imagination: AUDITORY	V3		OPEN THINKING	To Trigger Imagination: VISUAL

DIFFERENCES TO NAVIGATE

- People who use the AKV pattern may inadvertently hurt someone who uses the VKA pattern with their verbal sarcasm; try not to take it personally.
- Those who use the AKV pattern are visually sensitive, so someone with a VKA pattern should avoid overloading them with too much visual information like long emails and complex visual directions.
- While it's natural for the VKA pattern to hold steady eye contact, it isn't for the AKV pattern, so don't force it—sit next to (not across from) each other to avoid uncomfortable eye contact.

CREATING CONDITIONS TO GROW RESPECT

- If you each want to know how the other feels, it's best to take a walk or be on your feet as you talk through feelings or complicated issues.
- People who use the VKA pattern will naturally talk in circles and ask a great deal of questions. Someone who uses the AKV pattern will dominate the conversation if all questions are answered, so instead say something like, "What a good question, what do *you* think?"
- Those who use the AKV pattern will be tempted to interrupt or finish sentences for someone who uses the VKA pattern. Practice verbal patience by noticing body sensations and breath, being aware that people who use the VKA pattern are especially sensitive to tone of voice.
- Those who use the AKV pattern have a lot of intensity behind their words. Those with the VKA pattern need to recognize this as the passion behind their words, and not necessarily directed at them.
- Try to *do* things—be in action with each other as much as possible.
- It is most natural for people with the AKV pattern to *express* love through words and actions; they are deeply touched by and sensitive to a short caring note or image. It is most natural for those who use the VKA pattern to express love by showing, writing, and demonstrating through actions. Caring words and tone of voice impact them deeply.

VAK⇔KVA

DIFFERENCES TO NAVIGATE

- People who use the KVA pattern tend to be very independent and can grasp physical and technical tasks quickly. Refrain

Visual, Auditory, and Kinesthetic VAK PATTERN			Kinesthetic, Visual, and Auditory KVA PATTERN		
V1	FOCUSED THINKING	To Trigger Concentration: VISUAL	**K1**	FOCUSED THINKING	To Trigger Concentration: KINESTHETIC
A2	SORTING THINKING	To Trigger Sorting: AUDITORY	**V2**	SORTING THINKING	To Trigger Sorting: VISUAL
K3	OPEN THINKING	To Trigger Imagination: KINESTHETIC	**A3**	OPEN THINKING	To Trigger Imagination: AUDITORY

from showing and telling them what to do; they generally prefer to figure things out on their own.

- Those who use the VAK pattern should not assume they know what someone who uses the KVA pattern is feeling by looking at their facial expression, which may be flat. This is not necessarily an indication that they are angry or bored. It's easy to know what someone who uses the VAK pattern is feeling because it's written all over their face.

- Those who use the VAK pattern need to allow for periods of silence and reflection when communicating with someone who uses the auditorily sensitive KVA pattern and shouldn't try to finish sentences.

- Those who use the KVA pattern should keep in mind that those who use the VAK pattern are sensitive to physical touch and movement; a punch to the shoulder in jest, for example, may be misinterpreted.

CREATING CONDITIONS TO GROW RESPECT

- To communicate it's best if you both are looking at the same thing; therefore use a common visual whenever possible. If you are apart, try using webcams or Skype with screen share.

- Those who use the KVA pattern will be more comfortable when moving around while someone with the VAK pattern talks.

- Those who use the KVA pattern may get frustrated with a

person with the VAK pattern's lengthy stories. Create a kinesthetic cue you can use to remind the other to include you in
the conversation, like putting your hand gently on their back.

- To verbally disagree effectively, let the person who uses the
KVA pattern write their feelings first while listening to relaxing music and then be able to move while talking. The person
who uses the VAK pattern should go on a slow walk first,
and then come back to the conversation with a slowed tempo.

- For the person who uses the VAK pattern it really helps to
talk things out. For someone who uses the KVA pattern it
helps to write or draw things out.

- If you want someone who uses the KVA pattern to share
their feelings, request they write or draw them for you first,
then share them. Physical comfort is very important to them.
If you want someone who uses the VAK pattern to share
their feelings, ask them to go on a slow walk in an environment where they can relax.

- People who use the VAK pattern can be inspiring and add
vitality to the ability of someone who uses the KVA pattern
to make something happen.

- It's most natural for a person who uses the KVA pattern to
express love through actions and showing the other person
visually. It's most natural for someone with the VAK pattern
to express love by writing and telling the other person. They
will be deeply affected by touch.

VAK⇔KAV

Visual, Auditory, and Kinesthetic VAK PATTERN				Kinesthetic, Auditory, and Visual KAV PATTERN			
V1	👁	FOCUSED THINKING	To Trigger Concentration: VISUAL	K1	✋	FOCUSED THINKING	To Trigger Concentration: KINESTHETIC
A2	👂	SORTING THINKING	To Trigger Sorting: AUDITORY	A2	👂	SORTING THINKING	To Trigger Sorting: AUDITORY
K3	✋	OPEN THINKING	To Trigger Imagination: KINESTHETIC	V3	👁	OPEN THINKING	To Trigger Imagination: VISUAL

DIFFERENCES TO NAVIGATE

- People who use the KAV pattern will be very prone to give hugs, and engage in other physical touch or activity. They may not understand that someone who uses the VAK pattern is inclined to sit still for long periods.
- A person who uses the VAK pattern organizes with lists and likes visual order, while someone who uses the KAV pattern organizes in piles and functionally for what will be needed to accomplish a certain task.
- It's important for someone who uses the VAK pattern to understand how important "feeling good" and physical comfort are to someone who uses the KAV pattern when it comes to their space, surroundings, and clothing.
- Someone who uses the VAK pattern can overwhelm a person who has the KAV pattern with visual details. Therefore, communicate as much as possible verbally, although if you want to praise them, a short card will have a huge impact.
- A person who uses the VAK pattern needs to not insist on direct and steady eye contact with another who has the KAV pattern—instead, sit next to them instead of across from them.

CREATING CONDITIONS TO GROW RESPECT

- As the person who uses the VAK pattern shares an inspiring vision, the person who uses the KAV pattern naturally figures out how to turn it into concrete action.
- If you find yourself arguing, suggest going for a walk to talk it out. Likewise, to share feelings, try going for a long, slow walk at a relaxed pace. Use metaphors with each other to describe how you are feeling. It's also quite effective for you to talk while sitting back-to-back.
- It's most natural for someone who uses the VAK pattern to express their love by writing and telling you how they feel. They will be deeply affected by touch.

- The most natural way for someone who uses the KAV pattern to express their love will be in actions and through words. They will be deeply affected by a short note.

VAK⇔VKA

Visual, Auditory, and Kinesthetic VAK PATTERN			
V1	👁	**FOCUSED THINKING**	To Trigger Concentration: **VISUAL**
A2	🗣	**SORTING THINKING**	To Trigger Sorting: **AUDITORY**
K3	✋	**OPEN THINKING**	To Trigger Imagination: **KINESTHETIC**

Visual, Kinesthetic, and Auditory VKA PATTERN			
V1	👁	**FOCUSED THINKING**	To Trigger Concentration: **VISUAL**
K2	✋	**SORTING THINKING**	To Trigger Sorting: **KINESTHETIC**
A3	🗣	**OPEN THINKING**	To Trigger Imagination: **AUDITORY**

DIFFERENCES TO NAVIGATE

- When arguing, be aware that people who use the VKA pattern are very sensitive to tone of voice. Ask them to write about how they feel before talking it through or to take notes on the conversation.
- Be aware that someone who uses the VAK pattern does not like to move as quickly as a person with the VKA pattern does. Going at one's own rhythm is important to them.
- People who use the VAK pattern are sensitive to physical touch; having a meaningful conversation while rubbing their feet or back increases their receptivity.
- Someone who uses the VAK pattern will want to talk things through; the VKA pattern will need to move while listening to stay engaged.

CREATING CONDITIONS TO GROW RESPECT

- You are both born visual collaborators—and may enjoy sharing images, or having conversations about movies and books.
- How things look is very important to both of you.

- Communicate as much as possible in writing—email, notes, cards, and letters—or face-to-face, including Skype, etc.
- It's most natural for a person who uses the VAK pattern to express their love by writing and telling you how they feel. They will be deeply affected by touch, objects with meaning, or actions done on their behalf.
- It is natural for a person who uses the VKA pattern to express their love by showing you with actions. Words, tone of voice, and music touch them deeply.

VAK⇔AKV

Visual, Auditory, and Kinesthetic VAK PATTERN			Auditory, Kinesthetic, and Visual AKV PATTERN		
V1	FOCUSED THINKING	To Trigger Concentration: VISUAL	A1	FOCUSED THINKING	To Trigger Concentration: AUDITORY
A2	SORTING THINKING	To Trigger Sorting: AUDITORY	K2	SORTING THINKING	To Trigger Sorting: KINESTHETIC
K3	OPEN THINKING	To Trigger Imagination: KINESTHETIC	V3	OPEN THINKING	To Trigger Imagination: VISUAL

DIFFERENCES TO NAVIGATE

- People who use the AKV pattern are visually sensitive, and someone who uses the VAK pattern may, without realizing it, overwhelm them with eye contact, detailed information—emails, written memos, visual directions.
- A person who uses the AKV pattern may misunderstand, disregard, or make fun of the need for visual tidiness of a person who uses the VAK pattern.
- Allow the eyes of a person who uses the AKV pattern to wander rather than interpreting it as a sign of disrespect or lack of interest.
- A person who uses the AKV pattern is naturally verbally directive, while someone with the VAK pattern is naturally verbally explorative. Unaware of this dynamic, a person with an

AKV pattern may want another with the VAK pattern to get to the point quickly.

CREATING CONDITIONS TO GROW RESPECT

- If arguing with someone who uses the AKV pattern becomes too verbally intense for a person who uses the VAK pattern, it would help him or her to move around; it will enable the person who uses the VAK pattern to know what really matters to them, and help a person with the AKV pattern to have patience with those who speak more slowly.
- People who use either of the two patterns share the ability and desire to speak passionately about what matters to them.
- A person who uses the VAK pattern will find taking notes and making lists to be the easiest way to keep track of what is said and what needs to be done. But don't expect a person who uses the AKV pattern to necessarily read or follow the notes.
- Make sure there is time for the two of you to talk through a task to make sure expectations are clear before beginning it.
- Verbal banter will come easily to both of you. To express feelings to each other, slow down verbally and include touch or walking together.
- It is most natural for a person who uses the AKV pattern to express love through words, actions, and objects; a short caring note or image will have a deep effect on them.
- It's most natural for a person who uses the VAK pattern to express their love by writing and talking about how they feel. They will be deeply affected by touch.

VAK⇔AVK

DIFFERENCES TO NAVIGATE

- A person who uses the AVK pattern may use a sharper tone of voice or be directive with their words.

Visual, Auditory, and Kinesthetic **VAK PATTERN**		
V1 👁	**FOCUSED THINKING**	To Trigger Concentration: **VISUAL**
A2 👂	**SORTING THINKING**	To Trigger Sorting: **AUDITORY**
K3 ✋	**OPEN THINKING**	To Trigger Imagination: **KINESTHETIC**

Auditory, Visual, and Kinesthetic **AVK PATTERN**		
A1 👂	**FOCUSED THINKING**	To Trigger Concentration: **AUDITORY**
V2 👁	**SORTING THINKING**	To Trigger Sorting: **VISUAL**
K3 ✋	**OPEN THINKING**	To Trigger Imagination: **KINESTHETIC**

- Someone who uses the VAK pattern may sound wishy-washy or on the fence to another who uses the AVK pattern.
- Someone who uses the AVK pattern may overlook visual details that are important to someone who uses the VAK pattern.

CREATING CONDITIONS TO GROW RESPECT

- You are comfortable partners, particularly in brainstorming situations when ideas are flying.
- A person who uses the AVK pattern is very good at seeing the big picture and details at the same time.
- Both of you may be slow to move into action or may struggle to discover what concretely to do. You may need to bring in outside support to help you get things done together.
- The two of you meet naturally in verbal repartee, but be aware that when you get going, you could take up all the airspace of a conversation that includes others.
- To share how you feel, you both will have to first spend time on your own, getting in touch with your own emotions, before expressing them. To receive each other, try taking a walk or going for a drive.
- It is most natural for a person who uses the VAK pattern and another who uses the AVK pattern to express their love through words or writing to each other; both like to have physical space around them. Touch is private and may be deeply felt.

VKA⇔KVA

Visual, Kinesthetic, and Auditory VKA PATTERN				Kinesthetic, Visual, and Auditory KVA PATTERN			
V1		FOCUSED THINKING	To Trigger Concentration: VISUAL	K1		FOCUSED THINKING	To Trigger Concentration: KINESTHETIC
K2		SORTING THINKING	To Trigger Sorting: KINESTHETIC	V2		SORTING THINKING	To Trigger Sorting: VISUAL
A3		OPEN THINKING	To Trigger Imagination: AUDITORY	A3		OPEN THINKING	To Trigger Imagination: AUDITORY

DIFFERENCES TO NAVIGATE

- Sometimes people who use the KVA pattern can be frustrating for a person who uses the VKA pattern because they work so independently. Be aware that you may prefer different levels of interaction, including social events that someone with the KVA pattern may not want to attend.
- A person who uses the KVA pattern may overlook visual details that are important to someone with the VKA pattern.
- People who use the VKA pattern may not be aware how important "feeling good" is to others who use the KVA pattern. This includes comforting physical space and surroundings.

CREATING CONDITIONS TO GROW RESPECT

- You are good partners since you both are auditorily sensitive; you communicate naturally with each other via notes and move smoothly together into action. You are both comfortable with long silences.
- Because you are both auditorily sensitive, you tend not to offend or upset each other with your words, and are comfortable communicating in writing as well as speaking to each other. You both may imagine what the other is thinking

or feeling, however, and not speak about it unless you are moving or in action.

- You will find that organizing space comes naturally to you both; a person with the VKA pattern will be more concerned with looks, whereas a person who uses the KVA pattern is more concerned with comfort and function.
- Tone of voice and certain words can have a meaningful lasting impact for you both.
- Individuals with these patterns do well creating things together and are good at helping each other concretely visualize ideas.
- It may be easier to gesture or hug each other when you want to let the other person know you care or are sorry.
- It is most natural for people with the VKA and KVA patterns to express love through actions, and showing or writing to each other. Spoken words and tone of voice can have a deep and long-lasting effect on the other.

VKA⇔KAV

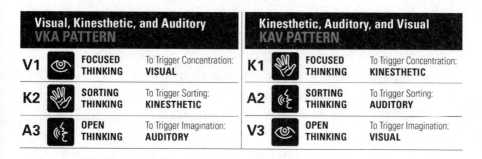

Visual, Kinesthetic, and Auditory VKA PATTERN				Kinesthetic, Auditory, and Visual KAV PATTERN			
V1		FOCUSED THINKING	To Trigger Concentration: VISUAL	K1		FOCUSED THINKING	To Trigger Concentration: KINESTHETIC
K2		SORTING THINKING	To Trigger Sorting: KINESTHETIC	A2		SORTING THINKING	To Trigger Sorting: AUDITORY
A3		OPEN THINKING	To Trigger Imagination: AUDITORY	V3		OPEN THINKING	To Trigger Imagination: VISUAL

DIFFERENCES TO NAVIGATE

- A person who uses the VKA pattern will organize their space by the way things look, whereas someone who uses the KAV pattern will organize by piles or function.
- Someone who uses the VKA pattern has to be careful not to

overwhelm with visual information someone who uses the KAV pattern; it will be more effective to communicate as much as possible verbally.

- While it's natural for a person who uses the VKA pattern to make steady eye contact, it is not comfortable for someone who uses the KAV pattern, so don't force it. Sit next to (not across from) them or walk in nature side by side so their eyes can move where they want to.
- A person who uses the VKA pattern tends to ask a lot of questions, which might annoy someone with the KAV pattern who prefers to talk about experiences and actions taken.

CREATING CONDITIONS TO GROW RESPECT

- If someone who uses the VKA pattern is in a conflict with someone who uses the KAV pattern, walking while talking, especially out of doors, will help both find words that align with feelings and needs.
- You two can partner well, particularly when creating something concrete that requires specific action or traveling.
- If you are discussing something with a person who uses the KAV pattern, allow them to move around so they can pay attention better and contribute more.
- A person who uses the VKA pattern can be a stimulating partner for someone with the KAV pattern because they can collaborate with visual and kinesthetic detail.
- A person who uses the KAV pattern should be aware that people who use the VKA pattern have sensitive ears; whenever possible, walk and talk, particularly for important information.
- It is most natural for a person who uses the VKA pattern to express love by showing, writing, and demonstrating through actions.
- It is most natural for a person with the KAV pattern to express his or her love in actions and words.

VKA⇔AVK

Visual, Kinesthetic, and Auditory VKA PATTERN			Auditory, Visual, and Kinesthetic AVK PATTERN		
V1	FOCUSED THINKING	To Trigger Concentration: VISUAL	A1	FOCUSED THINKING	To Trigger Concentration: AUDITORY
K2	SORTING THINKING	To Trigger Sorting: KINESTHETIC	V2	SORTING THINKING	To Trigger Sorting: VISUAL
A3	OPEN THINKING	To Trigger Imagination: AUDITORY	K3	OPEN THINKING	To Trigger Imagination: KINESTHETIC

NAVIGATING DIFFERENCES

- A person who uses the VKA mind pattern will be less likely to take a person with the AVK pattern's curt tone of voice or message personally if they are moving while listening or playing with something in their hands.
- The verbal stamina of a person who uses the AVK pattern can be overwhelming for someone with the VKA pattern unless he or she is moving or writing down what is said.
- People who use these two patterns can prearrange a hand gesture to remind the person with the AVK pattern to make space for one with the VKA pattern to speak.
- A person who uses the VKA pattern needs to be sensitive to how difficult it can be for another with the AVK pattern to do complex physical tasks.

CREATING CONDITIONS TO GROW RESPECT

- Encourage each other to communicate as much as possible via notes, email, and texts.
- When sharing something meaningful with a person who uses the VKA pattern, be aware that they are auditorily sensitive, especially to tone of voice.
- Since a person who uses the VKA pattern tends to speak with one question after the other, people who use the AVK pattern

can become frustrated listening and want them to "get to the point." They should avoid finishing the other's sentences for them.

- A person who uses the VKA pattern asks questions that help people who use the AVK pattern sort through their feelings, especially if they are walking together, or if the spoken words are written down on a piece of paper both can see.

- It is most natural for a person who uses the VKA pattern to express love by showing, writing, and demonstrating through actions. Words spoken with love will have a deep effect on them.

- It is most natural for one with the AVK pattern to express love through spoken words, then in writing. Touch will have a deep, lasting effect on them.

KAV⇔KVA

Kinesthetic, Auditory, and Visual KAV PATTERN				Kinesthetic, Visual, and Auditory KVA PATTERN		
K1		FOCUSED THINKING	To Trigger Concentration: KINESTHETIC	K1	FOCUSED THINKING	To Trigger Concentration: KINESTHETIC
A2		SORTING THINKING	To Trigger Sorting: AUDITORY	V2	SORTING THINKING	To Trigger Sorting: VISUAL
V3		OPEN THINKING	To Trigger Imagination: VISUAL	A3	OPEN THINKING	To Trigger Imagination: AUDITORY

NAVIGATING DIFFERENCES

- Because people who use the KVA pattern have such sensitive ears, visual communication or speaking while walking in nature is the most effective. Their words are usually expressed softly and slowly.

- A person with the KAV pattern may be sensitive to what someone with the KVA pattern writes or shows them and become easily overwhelmed by too much visual input, which can have a profound effect on them.

CREATING CONDITIONS TO GROW RESPECT

- People whose minds use these two patterns are great partners in physical activity and can work well together on concrete projects of all sorts.
- To get through to someone who uses the KVA pattern, it's most effective for a person who uses the KAV pattern to ask him or her to take notes while listening in order to pay more focused attention.
- Physical contact will be very casual for people with either of these two patterns, and talking about your feelings while doing something will come more easily.
- You both tend to organize in piles, so shared space will be easy.
- Physical comfort in your environment will be important for both of you.
- It is most natural for a person with the KAV pattern to express love in actions and words. It is most natural for one who uses the KVA pattern to express their love in actions and showing or writing to another person.

KAV⇔AKV

Kinesthetic, Auditory, and Visual KAV PATTERN			Auditory, Kinesthetic, and Visual AKV PATTERN		
K1	FOCUSED THINKING	To Trigger Concentration: KINESTHETIC	A1	FOCUSED THINKING	To Trigger Concentration: AUDITORY
A2	SORTING THINKING	To Trigger Sorting: AUDITORY	K2	SORTING THINKING	To Trigger Sorting: KINESTHETIC
V3	OPEN THINKING	To Trigger Imagination: VISUAL	V3	OPEN THINKING	To Trigger Imagination: VISUAL

NAVIGATING DIFFERENCES

- People who use the AKV pattern may have trouble doing concrete things in the systematic way that someone with the

KAV pattern does, and may have trouble estimating how much time something will take.

- A person who uses the KAV pattern may sound wishy-washy and on the fence to a person with the AKV pattern, who may sound directive and overly authoritative to the person with the KAV pattern.

CREATING CONDITIONS TO GROW RESPECT

- Detailed visual tasks such as paying bills may be difficult for both people.
- Since both patterns are visually sensitive, they connect most comfortably auditorily and kinesthetically, in words, music, and action.
- Their shared space will likely be organized more by function than by the way it looks.
- Being engaged in shared physical activity while talking about a joint vision works very well for both.
- People with either of these patterns may tend to have a deep unconscious image of the way things will look when complete. It's necessary therefore to talk it over to make sure it's the same thing or destination.
- Actions, experiences, and spoken words will be the most natural ways to express love, while writing each other short notes will have a deep and meaningful impact.

KAV⇔AVK

Kinesthetic, Auditory, and Visual KAV PATTERN				Auditory, Visual, and Kinesthetic AVK PATTERN			
K1		FOCUSED THINKING	To Trigger Concentration: KINESTHETIC	A1		FOCUSED THINKING	To Trigger Concentration: AUDITORY
A2		SORTING THINKING	To Trigger Sorting: AUDITORY	V2		SORTING THINKING	To Trigger Sorting: VISUAL
V3		OPEN THINKING	To Trigger Imagination: VISUAL	K3		OPEN THINKING	To Trigger Imagination: KINESTHETIC

NAVIGATING DIFFERENCES

- People who use the AVK pattern can have difficulty doing physical tasks, while people who use the KAV pattern love the concrete world of action.
- Someone with the AVK pattern prefers to live in the world of abstract ideas and may get frustrated or confused by a person with the KAV pattern's action-first attitude and preference for talk about the concrete and experiential.

CREATING CONDITIONS TO GROW RESPECT

- A person who uses the KAV pattern can be helpful moving someone with the AVK pattern's ideas into specific action.
- Both patterns are best communicating as much as possible verbally, except when a deep connection is desired. In that case, it should be brief.
- Sit next to (not across from) each other so the person with the KAV pattern's shy eyes can move where they want to.
- If someone who uses the AVK pattern is in conflict with a person who uses the KAV pattern, walk-and-talks can be very helpful so both can look where they want and discover what is needed.
- A person who uses the KAV pattern will naturally express love through actions and words; one with the AVK pattern will naturally express love in what they say and show.

KVA⇔AKV

NAVIGATING DIFFERENCES

- With their quick-tongued sarcasm, people who use the AKV pattern can be unintentionally hurtful to others who use the KVA pattern, or their verbal mastery can also be compelling and mesmerizing.

Kinesthetic, Visual, and Auditory KVA PATTERN		
K1	FOCUSED THINKING	To Trigger Concentration: KINESTHETIC
V2	SORTING THINKING	To Trigger Sorting: VISUAL
A3	OPEN THINKING	To Trigger Imagination: AUDITORY

Auditory, Kinesthetic, and Visual AKV PATTERN		
A1	FOCUSED THINKING	To Trigger Concentration: AUDITORY
K2	SORTING THINKING	To Trigger Sorting: KINESTHETIC
V3	OPEN THINKING	To Trigger Imagination: VISUAL

- A person with the AKV pattern is visually sensitive, so another who uses the KVA pattern should communicate verbally with them as much as possible—by phone or face-to-face. Avoid long texts and emails.
- Someone who uses the KVA pattern tends to work independently and grasp physical and technical tasks quickly. Someone who uses the AKV pattern is a natural "coach" so they need to refrain from telling a KVA what to do or how to do it.
- A person who uses the KVA pattern is very sensitive to tone of voice and can be easily hurt by something someone who uses an AKV pattern says in jest.

CREATING CONDITIONS TO GROW RESPECT

- A person who uses the KVA pattern should stand or sit next to (rather than in front of) another with the AKV pattern so as to not force eye contact.
- If someone using the AKV pattern is talking too fast, a person using the KVA pattern can suggest that they get up and move around—it will enable them to know what really matters to them and to have patience with those who speak more slowly. The person with the AKV pattern needs to allow for a great deal of silence and try not to answer another person with the KVA pattern's questions, instead encouraging them to answer for themselves.

- Whenever possible, walk together when you have something important or sensitive to say.
- Give each other as much independence as you can and communicate as much as possible in writing, particularly if the topic is important.
- A person who uses the KVA pattern will naturally express their love in actions and by showing you, writing notes. A person who uses the AKV pattern will express love in words and actions.

KVA⇔AVK

Kinesthetic, Visual, and Auditory KVA PATTERN			Auditory, Visual, and Kinesthetic AVK PATTERN		
K1	FOCUSED THINKING	To Trigger Concentration: KINESTHETIC	A1	FOCUSED THINKING	To Trigger Concentration: AUDITORY
V2	SORTING THINKING	To Trigger Sorting: VISUAL	V2	SORTING THINKING	To Trigger Sorting: VISUAL
A3	OPEN THINKING	To Trigger Imagination: AUDITORY	K3	OPEN THINKING	To Trigger Imagination: KINESTHETIC

NAVIGATING DIFFERENCES

- People who use the AVK pattern can be verbally overwhelming to a person who uses the KVA mind pattern.
- Someone who uses the KVA pattern tends to be very independent and can grasp physical and technical tasks quickly and they generally prefer to figure things out on their own. A person who uses the AVK pattern should refrain from telling them what to do.
- An individual with the AVK pattern may find someone with the KVA pattern to be fidgety and be overwhelmed by their movement and need to get to action rather than discussing things.

- The person who uses the KVA pattern may overlook how sensitive the AVK pattern user can be in movement and physical tasks and not understand their reluctance to jump into action, and preference to sit and talk.

CREATING CONDITIONS TO GROW RESPECT

- The person who employs the AVK pattern has to be reminded to slow down their verbal tempo and give a user of the KVA pattern space to speak rather than interrupting to answer their questions or put words in their mouths. A simple prearranged signal, like a raised hand, can be helpful.
- To communicate feelings, a person who uses the KVA pattern may need time to write down what is most important before talking; it is more natural for them to move around and reflect on big questions first.
- To understand the feelings of someone who uses the AVK pattern, the person with the KVA pattern can write out very specific and open questions and offer a walk to discuss them.
- These two patterns can be a dynamic duo, with the person with the KVA pattern taking action and the one who follows the AVK pattern articulating what needs to be done.
- Shared space will come together aesthetically, especially if the AVK pattern follower lets the KVA user organize. They are best looking over things together, then moving them around.
- A person who uses the KVA pattern will naturally express love through actions, gifts, and by showing or writing. Another who has the AVK pattern will naturally express their love through what they say and show you.

AVK⇔AKV

Auditory, Visual, and Kinesthetic AVK PATTERN			Auditory, Kinesthetic, and Visual AKV PATTERN		
A1	**FOCUSED THINKING**	To Trigger Concentration: **AUDITORY**	**A1**	**FOCUSED THINKING**	To Trigger Concentration: **AUDITORY**
V2	**SORTING THINKING**	To Trigger Sorting: **VISUAL**	**K2**	**SORTING THINKING**	To Trigger Sorting: **KINESTHETIC**
K3	**OPEN THINKING**	To Trigger Imagination: **KINESTHETIC**	**V3**	**OPEN THINKING**	To Trigger Imagination: **VISUAL**

NAVIGATING DIFFERENCES

- People who use the AVK pattern are kinesthetically sensitive, so people who use the AKV pattern should avoid casual contact—punches on the arm, pats on the shoulder—and be aware that doing anything physical can be challenging for people who use the AVK pattern.

- A person who uses the AVK pattern will not be as comfortable talking about how they feel as another who has the AKV pattern.

- Both of these patterns are skillful and articulate verbally, but they can get carried away with verbal arguments when the AKV pattern user speaks with a great deal of emotion while the AVK pattern user speaks with precise and condescending language.

CREATING CONDITIONS TO GROW RESPECT

- Stand or sit next to (rather than in front of) a person who uses the AKV pattern so they can move their eyes where they want to.

- To share feelings, people with either pattern can get more receptive to each other by doodling and taking a few notes (AVK) or moving around (AKV) first. Talking comes natu-

rally who uses both patterns, but it is the least receptive mode
for both as well.

- You meet naturally in verbal repartee, but when the two of
  you get going, you could take up all the airspace in a conversation that involves others.
- A person who uses the AKV pattern will naturally express
  love in words and actions, the AVK person in words and by
  showing you. Touch is relaxing to someone with the AKV
  pattern but much more sensitive and meaningful to a person
  who uses the AVK pattern.

APPRECIATIONS TO
THE POSSIBILISTS

Whose hands were always on our backs:
Andy Bryner and David Peck

Whose hands guided us:
Milton Erickson, M.D.
Richard Kuboyama
Edith and William Mechanic
Sapiro family
Dr. Peter and Jeri McArthur
Heather McArthur and John Stevenson
Cuddihy family
Laver family
Morgan and Brendan Dewan
Dall family

Whose hands midwifed this book:
Julie Grau
Marnie Cochran
Mary Jane Ryan
Hamilton South

Whose hands supported us:

Georgi Abelanda

Joan Selix Berman

Suzy Amis Cameron

Al Carey

Jeff Dunn

Pat Dunn

Lorraine Tamaribuchi

Coleen Sotomayer

Robin Marrouche

Jacki Zehner

John Vieceli

Jim and Analea Holland, Trece Swanson, Alex Stoy, Scott Bonz, John Bresee, Tina Nardi, Erin Hirtle, Sara Bresee, Corinne Dyke, Greg and Steve Mayer, Monty and Sally Lutzker

Whom our hands bless:

Ana Li McIlraith

Elspeth and Gracie Stevenson

Ayla and Kai Cuddihy

Kate, Taylor, Hunter, Logan Kessler

Luke Dewan

Hannah Lutzker

Rose, Claire, Jasper, Quinn Cameron

Telebus, Hula, Mobi

BIBLIOGRAPHY

Ackerman, Diane. *An Alchemy of Mind: The Marvel and Mystery of the Brain.* New York: Scribner, 2004.

Angelou, Maya. *I Know Why the Caged Bird Sings.* New York: Penguin Random House, 2009.

Annis, Barbara, and Keith Merron. *Gender Intelligence: Breakthrough Strategies for Increasing Diversity and Improving Your Bottom Line.* New York: Harper Business, 2014.

Banks, Amy, M.D., and Leigh Ann Hirschman. *Four Ways to Click: Revise Your Brain for Stronger, More Rewarding Relationships.* New York: Tarcher, 2015.

Begley, Sharon. *Train Your Mind, Change Your Brain: How a New Science Reveals Our Extraordinary Potential to Transform Ourselves.* New York: Ballantine Books, 2007.

Bloom, Charlie, and Linda Bloom. *Happily Ever After . . . and 39 Other Myths about Love: Breaking Through to the Relationship of Your Dreams.* Novato, CA: New World Library, 2016.

Boorstein, Seymour. *Who's Talking Now: The Owl or the Crocodile.* Bloomington, IN: Author House, 2011.

Buckingham, Marcus, and Donald O. Clifton. *Now, Discover Your Strengths.* New York: Free Press, 2001.

Commission on Children at Risk. *Hardwired to Connect: The New Scientific Case for Authoritative Communities.* New York: Institute for American Values, 2003.

Cooperrider, David, Diana Whitney, and Jacqueline Stavros. *The Appreciative Inquiry Handbook: For Leaders of Change.* Oakland, CA: Berrett-Koehler, 2003.

Covey, Stephen R. *The Speed of Trust: The One Thing That Changes Everything.* New York: Free Press, 2006.

Davidson, Richard, Ph.D., and Sharon Begley. *The Emotional Life of Your*

Brain: How Its Unique Patterns Affect the Way You Think, Feel, and Live—and How You Can Change Them. New York: Hudson Street Press, 2012.

Desimone, R. "Neural Synchrony and Selective Attention." International Joint Conference on Neural Networks, 2009, 683–84.

Dobson, Terry, and Victor Miller. *Aikido in Everyday Life: Giving In to Get Your Way.* Berkeley, CA: North Atlantic Books, 1994.

Doidge, Norman. *The Brain That Changes Itself: Stories of Personal Triumph from the Frontiers of Brain Science.* New York: Penguin Books, 2007.

Dweck, Carol. *Mindset: The New Psychology of Success.* New York: Random House, 2006.

Frankl, Viktor E. *Man's Search for Meaning.* New York: Pocket Books, 1997.

Fuller, R. Buckminster, Jerome Agel, and Quentin Fiore. *I Seem to Be a Verb.* N.p.: Gingko Press, 2016.

Gallwey, Timothy. *The Inner Game of Work.* New York: Random House, 2000.

Goleman, Daniel. *Social Intelligence: The New Science of Human Relationships.* New York: Bantam Books, 2001.

Hawkins, Jeff, and Sandra Blakeslee. *On Intelligence: How a New Understanding of the Brain Will Lead to the Creation of Truly Intelligent Machines.* New York: Times Books, 2004.

Herrmann, Ned. *The Creative Brain.* Lake Lure, NC: Brain Books, 1995.

Hillman, James. *The Soul's Code: In Search of Character and Calling.* New York: Random House, 1996.

Hock, Dee W. *Birth of the Chaordic Age.* Oakland, CA: Berrett-Koehler, 2000.

Huffington, Arianna. *Thrive: The Third Metric to Redefining Success and Creating a Life of Well-Being, Wisdom, and Wonder.* New York: Harmony Books, 2015.

Isaacson, Walter. *Einstein: His Life and Universe.* New York: Simon & Schuster, 2008.

John, E. Roy. "Neurometric Evaluation of Brain Function in Normal & Learning Disabled Children." International Academy for Research in Learning Disabilities Monograph Series, no. 5. Ann Arbor: University of Michigan Press, 1989.

Kabat-Zinn, Jon. *Coming to Our Senses: Healing Ourselves and the World Through Mindfulness.* New York: Hyperion, 2005.

Kahneman, Daniel. *Thinking, Fast and Slow.* New York: Farrar, Straus & Giroux, 2011.

Kanter, Rosabeth Moss. "Collaborative Advantage: The Art of Alliances." *Harvard Business Review* 72, no. 4 (July–August 1994): 96–108.

Kounios, John, and Mark Beeman. "The Aha! Moment: The Neural Basis of Solving Problems." Creativity Post, November 11, 2011. www.creativitypost.com/science/the_aha_moment._the_cognitive_neuroscience_of_insight.

Krishnamurti, Jiddu. *Freedom from the Known.* Edited by Mary Lutyens. New York: Harper, 2009.

Langer, Ellen J. *Mindfulness.* Boston: Da Capo Press, 1989.

Lieberman, Matthew D. *Social: Why Our Brains Are Wired to Connect.* New York: Crown, 2013.

Markova, Dawna, Ph.D. "From Rut to River: Co-Creating a Possible Future."

In *The Fabric of the Future: Women Visionaries of Today Illuminate the Path to Tomorrow,* ed. M. J. Ryan. Berkeley, CA: Conari Press, 1998.

———. *I Will Not Die an Unlived Life: Reclaiming Purpose and Passion.* Berkeley, CA: Conari Press, 2000.

———. *The Open Mind: Exploring the 6 Patterns of Natural Intelligence.* Berkeley, CA: Conari Press, 1996.

———. *Random Acts of Kindness.* Berkeley, CA: Conari Press, 2002.

———. *Think-Ability.* Park City, UT: Professional Thinking Partners, 2002.

Markova, Dawna, Ph.D., and Andy Bryner. *An Unused Intelligence: Physical Thinking for 21st Century Leadership.* Berkeley, CA: Conari Press, 1996.

Markova, Dawna, Ph.D., and Angie McArthur. *Collaborative Intelligence: Thinking with People Who Think Differently.* New York: Spiegel & Grau, 2015.

Markova, Dawna, Ph.D., and Anne R. Powell. *How Your Child Is Smart: A Life-Changing Approach to Learning.* Berkeley, CA: Conari Press, 1992.

———. *Learning Unlimited: Using Homework to Engage Your Child's Natural Style of Intelligence.* Berkeley, CA: Conari Press, 1998.

May, Rollo. *Love and Will.* New York: Norton, 1969.

Miller, Jean B. *Toward a New Psychology of Women.* 2nd ed. Boston: Beacon Press, 2012.

Palmer, Parker. *A Hidden Wholeness: The Journey Toward an Undivided Life.* San Francisco: Jossey-Bass, 2004.

Palmer, Wendy. *The Intuitive Body: Discovering the Wisdom of Conscious Embodiment and Aikido.* 3rd ed. San Francisco: Blue Snake Books, 2008.

Paul, Annie Murphy. *The Cult of Personality: How Personality Tests Are Leading Us to Miseducate Our Children, Mismanage Our Companies, and Misunderstand Ourselves.* New York: Free Press, 2004.

Pinker, Steven. *How the Mind Works.* New York: Norton, 1997.

Pittman, Frank. *Private Lies: Infidelity and the Betrayal of Intimacy.* New York: Norton, 1990.

Ratey, John J. *A User's Guide to the Brain: Perception, Attention, and the Four Theaters of the Brain.* New York: Vintage, 2001.

Real, Terrence. *The New Rules of Marriage: What You Need to Know to Make Love Work.* New York: Ballantine Books, 2008.

Rosen, Sidney. *My Voice Will Go with You: The Teaching Tales of Milton H. Erickson.* New York: Norton, 1982.

Ryan, M. J., ed. *The Fabric of the Future: Women Visionaries of Today Illuminate the Path to Tomorrow.* Berkeley, CA: Conari Press, 1998.

———. *Trusting Yourself: How to Stop Feeling Overwhelmed and Live More Happily with Less Effort.* New York: Broadway Books, 2004.

Siegel, Daniel. *The Developing Mind: How Relationships and the Brain Interact to Shape Who We Are.* New York: Guilford Press, 1999.

Stone, Douglas, Bruce Patton, and Sheila Heen. *Difficult Conversations: How to Discuss What Matters Most.* New York: Penguin Books, 2010.

Stone, Linda. "Why Email Can Be Habit Forming." *Huffington Post,* November 17, 2011. www.huffingtonpost.com/linda-stone/why-email-can-be-habit-fo_b_324781.html?

Taylor, Shelly E. "Biobehavioral Responses to Stress in Females: Tend and Be-friend, Not Fight or Flight." *Psychological Review* 107, no. 3 (July 2000): 411–29.

Turkle, Sherry. *Alone Together: Why We Expect More from Technology and Less from Each Other*. New York: Basic Books, 2011.

———. *Reclaiming Conversation: The Power of Talk in a Digital Age*. New York: Penguin Press, 2015.

Tutu, Desmond. *No Future Without Forgiveness*. Colorado Springs, CO: Image Books, 2000.

Wallace, B. Alan, Ph.D. *The Attention Revolution: Unlocking the Power of the Focused Mind*. Somerville, MA: Wisdom, 2006.

INDEX

A

accepting, agreeing vs., 142
accountability/nonaccountability
   stories, 167, 170
achieving mastery, 123
Adapting (thinking talent)
   drivers-of-thinking map, *102*
   identifying talent of, *83*
   need represented by, *92*
   shadow attribute of, *91*
agreeing, accepting vs., 142
alpha waves, 21
amygdala, 99
analytic inquiry style
   characteristics of, *125, 127, 143*
   open questions, 135–36
   shadow questions, *130, 151*
analytic language of understanding,
   100
   characteristics of, *107*
   drivers-of-thinking map, *102*
   expressing intimacy and, *117*

giving advice and, *113*
   personal example, *110*
   stressful situations and, *115*
   time and money and, *114*
Angelou, Maya, xvi-xvii, 5, 142, 187
assessments. *See* mind mapping;
   self-assessment
attention, 4–15
   about, 4
   auditory input, 23, *24*
   being "lost in thought," 20
   certainties that keep your mind
      closed, 7
   daydreaming, 21
   differences as resources, 7–9
   discovery rather than certainty, 6–7
   focused attention, 20, 21, 55
   open attention, 20, 21–22, 55
   "paying attention," 5–6
   practice: Möbius strip, *14–15*, 72
   practice: reclaiming attention, *13–14*
   reclaiming, 4–13

attention (*cont.*)
  redirecting, 5
  sorting attention, 20, 21, 55
  states of, 20–23, *57–58*, 59
  trim tab analogy, 4–5
  Zinn's collective attention-deficit
    disorder, 5
auditory mind patterns
  AKV (auditory-kinesthetic-visual),
    28, 48–51, *48*
    characteristics, 50–51
    communication, 50–51
    message from someone who uses
      the AKV pattern, 49–50
    snapshot, 48–49
  AVK (auditory-visual-kinesthetic),
    28, 44–47, *44*
    characteristics, 46–47
    communication, 46–47
    message from someone who uses
      the AVK pattern, 45–46
    snapshot, 44–45
  communication and, 46–47, 50–51,
    60–61
  discovering your own mind pattern,
    25, *26–28*, 29
  interactions
    AVK⇔AKV, 215–16, *215*
    KAV⇔AKV, 209–10, *209*
    KAV⇔AVK, *210*, 211
    KVA⇔AKV, 211–13, *212*
    KVA⇔AVK, 213–14, *213*
    VAK⇔AKV, 201–2, *201*
    VAK⇔AVK, 202–3, *203*
    VKA⇔AKV, 67–71, 195–96,
      195
    VKA⇔AVK, 207–8, *207*
  misunderstandings leading to
    relational breakdowns, 55–56
  triggers, *60–61*

auditory thinking, 23, *24*
  mind patterns, 26–28, *58–59*
  self-assessment, 25, *26–28*, 29
auditory triggers, *60–61*

B
"being in the zone," 80
Believing (thinking talent)
  drivers-of-thinking map, *102*
  identifying talent of, *83*
  need represented by, *92*
  shadow attribute of, *91*
beta waves, 21
biases
  diminishing people's relational
    capacities, 7–9
  uncovering your own biases, 9–11, *11*
blame/choice stories, 166–67,
    169–70, 182–83
blessings, 190–92
blind spots, thinking talents, 105–6
bonding, 138–39, 142
  examples of bridging the gap,
    139–42, 145–50
Boorstein, Seymour, 99
brain
  amygdala, 99
  plasticity of, 122
brain-dominance surveys, 100
brain wave states, 20–21
bridging, 142, 144, 150, 152
bridging the gap, examples of,
    139–42, 145–50
Buckingham, Marcus, 80

C
choice/blame stories, 166–67,
    169–70, 182–83
"Clearness Committee" (process),
    136–37

Clifton, Donald O., 80
closing the eyes
  VAK mind pattern, 30
  VKA mind pattern, 33, 34
clothing
  AKV mind pattern, 67, 69
  KAV mind pattern, 37, 199
  VAK mind pattern, 30, 57
  VKA mind pattern, 33, 57
Collecting (thinking talent)
  drivers-of-thinking map, 102
  identifying talent of, 83
  need represented by, 92
  shadow attribute of, 91
collective attention-deficit disorder, 5
communication, xix, xix, 19–81
  biases about, 10
  breakdowns in, 19–20, 55–56,
    60–62
    reconciling differences, 20, 59,
      60–62, 62–72
  mind patterns
    AKV (auditory-kinesthetic-visual),
      50–51
    AVK (auditory-visual-kinesthetic),
      46–47
    KAV (kinesthetic-auditory-visual),
      37, 38–40
    KVA (kinesthetic-visual-auditory),
      43–44, 53, 54–55
    VAK (visual-auditory-kinesthetic),
      30, 31, 32–33, 53, 54–55
    VKA (visual-kinesthetic-auditory),
      35–36
  reconciling differences among mind
    patterns, 59, 60–62, 62–72
confusion, 123–24
connecting
  attention, 4–15
  reclaiming your attention, 4–9, 13

uncovering your own biases,
    9–11, 11
  as voyage of discovery, 6, 11–13
Connection (thinking talent)
  drivers-of-thinking map, 102
  identifying talent of, 84
  need represented by, 92
  shadow attribute of, 91
conscious state of mind, 20, 21
conscious thought, 22
control, rut stories, 164
converging, 123
Creating Intimacy (thinking
    talent)
  drivers-of-thinking map, 102
  identifying talent of, 83
  need represented by, 92
  shadow attribute of, 91
The Creative Brain (Herrmann),
    100
"crocodile," 99
curiosity, 77–78, 80, 99–100
  about other's language of
    understanding, 106–8
  about your own language of
    understanding, 100–101, 102,
    103–4

D
data, and stories we tell ourselves,
    160–62, 164
daydreaming, 21
differences, as resources rather than
    deficits, 7–9
"difficult" people, 7–10
Dillard, Annie, 157
discovery
  connecting as voyage of discovery,
    11–13
  relating as process of, 6

E
Einstein, Albert, 40, 121
emotions
 AVK mind pattern, 45–46
 VAK mind pattern, 30
Enrolling (thinking talent)
 drivers-of-thinking map, *102*
 identifying talent of, *84*
 need represented by, *92*
 shadow attribute of, *91*
Equalizing (thinking talent)
 drivers-of-thinking map, *102*
 identifying talent of, *84*
 need represented by, *92*
 shadow attribute of, *91*
Erickson, Milton, 20–21
expressing intimacy, 116, *117*
eye contact
 AKV mind pattern, 49, 50, 195,
  201, 206, 212
 AVK mind pattern, 45
 KAV mind pattern, 37, 65, 67, 71,
  199
 KVA mind pattern, 41, 212
 VAK mind pattern, 32, 56, 57, 65,
  67, 71, 199, 201
 VKA mind pattern, 35, 56, 57, 195,
  206

F
Feeling for Others (thinking talent)
 drivers-of-thinking map, *102*
 identifying talent of, *84*
 need represented by, *92*
 shadow attribute of, *91*
fight-or-flight response, 99
Fixing It (thinking talent)
 drivers-of-thinking map, *102*
 identifying talent of, *84*

need represented by, *92*
 shadow attribute of, *91*
focused attention, 20, 21, *55*
Focusing (thinking talent)
 drivers-of-thinking map, *102*
 identifying talent of, *84*
 need represented by, *92*
 shadow attribute of, *91*
Forster, E.M., 3
Fuller, Buckminster, 4

G
Get to Action (thinking talent)
 drivers-of-thinking map, *102*
 identifying talent of, *85*
 need represented by, *93*
 shadow attribute of, *91*
Gladwell, Malcolm, 4
Goal Setting (thinking talent)
 drivers-of-thinking map, *102*
 identifying talent of, *85*
 need represented by, *93*
 shadow attribute of, *91*
growing from each other, 187–93
 example, 190–92
 practice: letter writing, 187–89
growing together, 175, 179–85
growth, 157, 187

H
Hadamard, Jacques, 40
hand gestures
 AVK pattern, 45
 KAV mind pattern, 37
Having Confidence (thinking talent)
 drivers-of-thinking map, *102*
 identifying talent of, *85*
 need represented by, *93*
 shadow attribute of, *91*

HBDI, 100
Herrmann, Ned, 100, 101
"hidden wholeness" (Merton), 108
Holmes, Oliver Wendell, 138
Huffington, Arianna, 4
Humor (thinking talent)
  drivers-of-thinking map, *102*
  identifying talent of, *85*
  need represented by, *93*
  shadow attribute of, *91*

I
imagination, 158, 175–76
impossibility/possibility stories,
  165–66, 169
"in the zone," 80
Including (thinking talent)
  drivers-of-thinking map, *102*
  identifying talent of, *85*
  need represented by, *93*
  shadow attribute of, *91*
Innovation (thinking talent)
  drivers-of-thinking map, *102*
  identifying talent of, *85*
  need represented by, *93*
  shadow attribute of, *91*
innovative inquiry style
  characteristics of, 126, *127, 143*
  open questions, 135–36
  shadow questions, *130, 151*
innovative language of understanding,
  100
  characteristics of, *107*
  drivers-of-thinking map, *102*
  expressing intimacy and, *117*
  giving advice and, *113*
  personal example, *111*
  stressful situations and, *115*
  time and money and, *114*

inquiry style
  bonding, 139–42, 145
  bridging the gap, 139–42, 144, 145,
    150, 152
  characteristics of, 124–26, *127,*
    143
  example of learning, 131–33
  identifying another's inquiry style,
    141, 143–45, 151
  identifying your own style, 127–28,
    127, 144
  inviting the other into your style,
    144–45, 152
  learning from your own wisdom,
    133–34
  open questions, 134–35
  practice: Committee of One,
    136–37
  process of reconciliation, 144–45
  reconciling differences, 138–53
  shadow questions, 129–30, *130,*
    151–52, *151*
  shadow side of, 129–30, *130*
  working with, 128–29
  See also individual inquiry styles
interrupting others
  AKV mind pattern, 48–49, 196
  AVK mind pattern, 46–47
intimacy, expressing, 116, *117*
invalidation/validation stories, 166,
  169–70

K
Kabat-Zinn, Jon, 5
kinesthetic mind patterns
  communication and, 38–40, 43–44,
    53, 54–55, 60–61
  discovering your own mind pattern,
    25, 26–28, 29

kinesthetic mind patterns (*cont.*)
  interactions
    KAV⇔AKV, 209–10, *209*
    KAV⇔AVK, *210*, 211
    KAV⇔KVA, 208–9, *208*
    KVA⇔AKV, 211–13, *212*
    KVA⇔AVK, 213–14, *213*
    VAK⇔KAV, 64–65, *64*, *198*,
      199–200
    VAK⇔KVA, 196–98, *197*
    VKA⇔KAV, 64–65, *64*, 205–6,
      205
    VKA⇔KVA, 204–5, *204*
  KAV (kinesthetic-auditory-visual),
    28, 36–40, *36*
    characteristics, 38–40
    communication, 37, 38–40
    message from someone who uses
      the KAV pattern, 38
    snapshot, 36–38
  KVA (kinesthetic-visual-auditory),
    28, 40–44, *40*
    characteristics, 42–44
    communication, 43–44, 53, *54–55*
    message from someone who uses
      the KVA pattern, 42
    snapshot, 41–42
  misunderstandings leading to
    relational breakdowns, 56
  triggers, *60–61*
kinesthetic thinking, 24, *24*
  mind patterns, 26–28, *58–59*
  self-assessment, 25, 26–28, 29
kinesthetic triggers, *60–61*
Kopp, Sheldon, 29
Krishnamurti, Jiddu, *13*

L
languages of learning. *See* inquiry
  style

languages of thought, 23–24, *24*
  identifying your thinking talents,
    80–83, *83–89*, 89
  See also auditory thinking;
    kinesthetic thinking; visual
    thinking
languages of understanding, 100–101,
  102, 103–4
  blind spots, 105–6
  drivers-of-thinking map, *102*
  expressing intimacy and, 116, *117*
  giving advice and, 112, *113*
  identifying others' language of
    understanding, 106–8
  identifying your language of
    understanding, 101, *102*, 103–4
  map of, 106, *107*
  multilingual, 103
  reconciling differences, 108–18
  stressful situations and, 114–15,
    115
  time and money and, 113, *114*
  *See also individual languages of
    understanding*
learning, xix, *xix*, 121–24
  achieving mastery, 123
  biases about, 10
  confusion, 123–24
  example of, 131–33
  learning from your own wisdom,
    133–34
  open questions, 134–35
  See also inquiry style
Levine, Peter A., 52
Lieberman, Matthew D., 3
list making, VAK mind pattern, 30,
  199
listening
  AKV mind pattern, 48
  VKA mind pattern, 34

looking away
  KAV mind pattern, 37
  VAK mind pattern, 30
  VKA mind pattern, 33
"lost in thought," 20
Love of Learning (thinking talent)
  drivers-of-thinking map, *102*
  identifying talent of, *86*
  need represented by, *93*
  shadow attribute of, *91*
Loving Ideas (thinking talent)
  drivers-of-thinking map, *102*
  identifying talent of, *86*
  need represented by, *93*
  shadow attribute of, *91*

M
Making Order (thinking talent)
  drivers-of-thinking map, *102*
  identifying talent of, *86*
  need represented by, *93*
  shadow attribute of, *91*
"mental metabolism," 22
Mentoring (thinking talent)
  drivers-of-thinking map, *102*
  identifying talent of, *86*
  need represented by, *93*
  shadow attribute of, *91*
Merton, Thomas, 108
mind pattern maps
  mapping another person's, 56, 57–58, 59
  mapping your own, 25, *26–28*, 29
  See also auditory mind patterns;
    kinesthetic mind patterns; visual
    mind patterns
mind pattern pairs, interactions
  AVK⇔AKV, 215–16, *215*
  KAV⇔AKV, 209–10, *209*
  KAV⇔AVK, *210*, 211

KAV⇔KVA, 208–9, *208*
KVA⇔AKV, 211–13, *212*
KVA⇔AVK, 213–14, *213*
VAK⇔AKV, 201–2, *201*
VAK⇔AVK, 202–3, *203*
VAK⇔KAV, 64–65, *64*, 198, 199–200
VAK⇔KVA, 196–98, *197*
VAK⇔VKA, 200–201, *200*
VKA⇔AKV, 67–71, 195–96, *195*
VKA⇔AVK, 207–8, *207*
VKA⇔KAV, 64–65, *64*, 205–6, *205*
VKA⇔KVA, 204–5, *204*
mind patterns
  of authors of this book, 53, 54–55
  checklist, *57–58*
  described, 23–24, *24*, 52
  mapping another person's, 56, *57–58*, 59
  mapping your own, 25, *26–28*, 29
  maps, 29–51
  misunderstandings leading to
    relational breakdowns, 55–56
  reconciling differences
    VAK⇔KAV, 64–65, *64*
    VKA⇔AKV, 67–71
  self-assessment, 25, *26–28*, 29
  See also auditory mind patterns;
    kinesthetic mind patterns; mind
    pattern maps; mind pattern pairs;
    visual mind patterns
mistrust, 175–76
misunderstanding, 77–96
  best of your thinking missing, 79–80
  curiosity missing, 77–78, 80, 99
  lack of awareness of thinking
    talents, 80–83, *83–89*, 89
Möbius strip, practice, *14–15*, 72
money and time, dealing with, 113, *114*

monopolizing conversations, AVK
    pattern, 47
movement and activity
    KAV mind pattern, 38–39
    KVA mind pattern, 42, 43
    VKA mind pattern, 34, 35

N
nonaccountability/accountability
    stories, 167, 170
Now, Discover Your Strengths
    (Clifton & Buckingham), 80–81

O
open attention, 20, 21–22, 56
open questions, 134–35
"opening the hand of thought," 7
Optimism (thinking talent)
    drivers-of-thinking map, *102*
    identifying talent of, *86*
    need represented by, *93*
    shadow attribute of, *91*
Ortega y Gasset, José, 11
"our hidden wholeness" (Merton),
    108
Outliers (Gladwell), 3

P
Palmer, Parker, *136*
Pando story, 192
Particularize (thinking talent)
    drivers-of-thinking map, *102*
    identifying talent of, *86*
    need represented by, *93*
    shadow attribute of, *91*
Peacemaking (thinking talent)
    drivers-of-thinking map, *102*
    identifying talent of, *87*
    need represented by, *93*
    shadow attribute of, *91*

physical comfort
    AKV mind pattern, 67
    KAV mind pattern, 37, 199, 209
    KVA mind pattern, 41, 198, 204,
        205, 207, 209
    VAK mind pattern, *58*, 65
    VKA mind pattern, *58*
physical contact
    KAV mind pattern, 39
    VAK mind pattern, 30
physical energy
    AKV mind pattern, 48, 49
    KAV mind pattern, 36–37, 39
    KVA mind pattern, 197
    VKA mind pattern, 34
Pittman, Frank, 175
possibility/impossibility stories,
    165–66, 169
practices
    Committee of One (inquiry style),
        136–37
    letter writing (growing from each
        other), 187–89
    Möbius strip (attention), *14–15*, 72
    reclaiming attention, *13–14*
    What's Data? What's Story? (trust
        and stories), 162
Precision (thinking talent)
    drivers-of-thinking map, *102*
    identifying talent of, *87*
    need represented by, *93*
    shadow attribute of, *91*
procedural inquiry style
    characteristics of, 125, *127*, *143*
    open questions, 135–36
    shadow questions, *130*, *151*
procedural language of
    understanding, 100
    characteristics of, *107*
    drivers-of-thinking map, *102*

expressing intimacy and, *117*
giving advice and, *113*
personal example, *110*
stressful situations and, *115*
time and money and, *114*
projections, 185, 186, 187
Proust, Marcel, 33

R
rational thinking, xv
reality check, 179, 180
projections, 186
using, 180–85
reclaiming attention, 4–13
practice, *13–14*
*Reclaiming Conversation: The
Power of Talk in a Digital Age*
(Turkle), 6
reconciling differences, 11–13,
97–98
communication styles and, 20,
60–62, 62–72
definitions of, 11–12
examples: showing it in context,
62–72
inquiry style, 138–53
languages of understanding,
108–18
rules of, xviii-xix, 192–93
trusting, 175–86
understanding, 78
using mind pattern chart, 59, 60–62,
62–72
reframing stories, 169–70
relating
as process of discovery, 6, 11–13
use of word, 5
relational capacity
biases that diminish, 7–9
factors interfering with, 4

relational inquiry style
characteristics of, 126, *127*, *143*
open questions, 135–36
shadow questions, *130*, *151*
relational intelligence, xv
relational language of understanding,
100
characteristics of, *107*
drivers-of-thinking map, *102*
expressing intimacy and, *117*
giving advice and, *113*
personal example, *111*
stressful situations and, *115*
time and money and, *114*
relationship, use of word, 5–6
Reliability (thinking talent)
drivers-of-thinking map, *102*
identifying talent of, *87*
need represented by, *93*
shadow attribute of, *91*
Richards, M.C., 36
river stories, 163, *163*, 164
blame/choice story, 166–67, 169–70,
182–83
impossibility/possibility story,
165–66, 169
invalidation/validation story, 166,
169
nonaccountability/accountability
story, 167, 170
reframing rut stories into,
169–70
Rumi, 97
rut stories
blame/choice story, 166–67, 169–70,
182–83
defined, 163–64, *163*
fear of, 173–74
impossibility/possibility story, 165,
169

rut stories (*cont.*)
  invalidation/validation story, 166,
    169
  nonaccountability/accountability
    story, 167, 170
  reframing into river stories, 169–70

S
safety, 157, 168, 170
Salk, Jonas, 133
Salle, David, 98
sarcasm
  AKV mind pattern, 49, 195, 211
  VKA mind pattern, 195
Seeking Excellence (thinking talent)
  drivers-of-thinking map, *102*
  identifying talent of, 87
  need represented by, *93*
  shadow attribute of, *91*
self-assessment
  identifying stories you tell yourself,
    163–64
  identifying your inquiry style,
    127–28, *127*, 151
  identifying your mind pattern, 25,
    26–28, 29
  identifying your thinking talents,
    80–83, *83–89*, 89
self-criticism, 89–90
Senge, Peter, 19
shadow attributes, 90, 129
  examples of, 90
  thinking talents, *91*
shadow questions, inquiry style,
    129–30, *130*, 151–52, *151*
Shange, Ntozake, 44
silence, KVA mind pattern, 41, 212
*Social: Why Our Brains Are Wired to
    Connect* (Lieberman), 3
sorting attention, 20, 21, 55–56

speaking style, VAK mind
    pattern, 30
Standing Out (thinking talent)
  drivers-of-thinking map, *102*
  identifying talent of, 87
  need represented by, *93*
  shadow attribute of, *91*
states of attention, 20–23
  mind pattern checklist, *57–58*, 59
  triggers for, 23–24, *24*, 55
stories
  of blame/choice, 166–67, 169–70,
    182–83
  data and, 160–62, *164*
  examples, *164*, 170–73, *174*
  identifying stories you tell yourself,
    163–64
  of impossibility/possibility, 165–66,
    169
  inner mythology, 159
  of invalidation/validation, 166,
    169
  mapping our stories, 167–70
  of nonaccountability/accountability,
    167, 170
  reframing, 169–70
  river stories, 163, *163*, 164
  rut stories, 163–64, *163*, 173–74
  transforming our stories, 170–74
  we tell ourselves, 158–68
Storytelling (thinking talent)
  drivers-of-thinking map, *102*
  identifying talent of, 87
  need represented by, *93*
  shadow attribute of, *91*
Strategy (thinking talent)
  drivers-of-thinking map, *102*
  identifying talent of, 88
  need represented by, *93*
  shadow attribute of, *91*

stressful situations, dealing with, 114–15, *115*

T

Taking Charge (thinking talent)
  drivers-of-thinking map, *102*
  identifying talent of, *88*
  need represented by, *93*
  shadow attribute of, *91*
taking notes
  VAK mind pattern, 30
  VKA mind pattern, 33
theta waves, 21
Thibon, Gustave, xiii
Thinking Ahead (thinking talent)
  drivers-of-thinking map, *102*
  identifying talent of, *88*
  need represented by, *93*
  shadow attribute of, *91*
Thinking Alone (thinking talent)
  drivers-of-thinking map, *102*
  identifying talent of, *88*
  need represented by, *93*
  shadow attribute of, *91*
Thinking Back (thinking talent)
  drivers-of-thinking map, *102*
  identifying talent of, *88*
  need represented by, *93*
  shadow attribute of, *91*
Thinking Logically (thinking talent)
  drivers-of-thinking map, *102*
  identifying talent of, *88*
  need represented by, *93*
  shadow attribute of, *91*
thinking talents, 75–76
  awareness of, 80–83, *83–89*, 89
  "being in the zone," 80
  blind spots, 105–6
  generating energy, 81

identifying your own talents, 80–83, *83–89*, 90
internal coherence of, *95–96*
needs represented by, 92, *92–93*, *94–95*
shadow attributes, 90, *91*
value of hidden talents, 89–90, *91*
what energizes you, 80–82
thought, languages of. *See* languages of thought
time and money, 113, *114*
touch, 24
  AKV mind pattern, 202, 203, 216
  AVK mind pattern, 45, 46, 216
  KAV mind pattern, 17, 37, 38, 39, 65, 66, 199
  KVA mind pattern, 41, 43, 197, 198, 199
  VAK mind pattern, 30, 59, 197, 198, 199, 200, 201, 202, 203
trust, xix, *xix*, 167–74
  biases about, 10
  defined, 157
  examples, 176–85
  growing from each other, 187–93
  growing together, 175, 179–85
  mapping our stories, 167–70
  practice: "What's Data? What's Story?", 162
  projections, 185, 186
  reality check, 179, 180
  reclaiming your trust in yourself, 176–79
  reconciling differences, 175–86
  river stories, 163, *163*, 164
  rut stories, 163–64, *163*
  safety, 157, 168, 170
  shifting from growing apart to growing trust, 179–84

trust (*cont.*)
  stories we tell ourselves, 158–68
  transforming our stories, 170–74
Turkle, Sherry, 6

U
unconscious state of mind, 21, 22
understanding, xix, *xix*, 75–96
  biases about, 10
  defined, 76
  misunderstanding, 77–96
  thinking talents, 75–96
  See also languages of understanding

V
validation/invalidation stories, 166, 169
visual mind patterns
  communication and, 32–33, 35–36, *53, 54–55, 60–61*
  discovering your own, 25, *26–28*, 29
  interactions
    VAK⇔AKV, 201–2, *201*
    VAK⇔AVK, 202–3, *203*
    VAK⇔KAV, 64–65, *64, 198*, 199–200
    VAK⇔KVA, 196–98, *197*
    VAK⇔VKA, 200–201, *200*
    VKA⇔AKV, 67–71, *195–96, 195*
    VKA⇔AVK, 207–8, *207*
    VKA⇔KAV, 64–65, *64*, 205–6, *205*
    VKA⇔KVA, 204–5, *204*
  misunderstandings leading to relational breakdowns, 56
  triggers, *60–61*
VAK (visual-auditory-kinesthetic), *28*, 29–33, *29*

characteristics, 31–33
communication, 30, 31, 32–33, *53, 54–55*
message from someone who uses the VAK pattern, 31
snapshot, 30
VKA (visual-kinesthetic-auditory), *28*, 33–36, *33*
characteristics, 35–36
communication, 35–36
message from someone who uses the VKA pattern, 34–35
snapshot, 33–34
visual thinking, 23–24, *24*
mind patterns, 26–28, 58–59
self-assessment, 25, *26–28*, 29
visual triggers, *60–61*
vocabulary
  AKV mind pattern, 50, 51
  AVK mind pattern, 44–45
  KAV mind pattern, 37
  KVA mind pattern, 42
  VAK mind pattern, 30
  VKA mind pattern, 34

W
Wanting to Win (thinking talent)
  drivers-of-thinking map, *102*
  identifying talent of, *89*
  need represented by, *93*
  shadow attribute of, *91*
withdrawing, KVA mind pattern, 41
wonder, 6
  reclaiming, *13*
writing
  AKV mind pattern, 49–50
  KAV mind pattern, 37–38
  KVA mind pattern, 198
  VAK mind pattern, 199, 201

ABOUT THE AUTHORS

DAWNA MARKOVA, Ph.D., is the CEO emeritus of Professional Thinking Partners, an organization that teaches collaborative thinking to CEOs and senior executives around the world. Internationally known for her research in the fields of learning and perception, she is a former senior affiliate of the Society for Organizational Learning, originated at Massachusetts Institute of Technology's Sloan School of Management; author of *I Will Not Die an Unlived Life;* coauthor of the international bestseller *Random Acts of Kindness;* and, with Angie McArthur, coauthor of *Collaborative Intelligence: Thinking with People Who Think Differently.* She lives in Hawaii.

ANGIE MCARTHUR is CEO of Professional Thinking Partners, a family-owned and -run business known for fostering the understanding of intellectual differences. As an expert in communication and learning styles, she has been a Thinking Partner to individuals and facilitated leadership teams around the world to reach their potential. She is also cofounder of Smartwired and the Smart Parenting Revolution, organizations dedicated to helping youth and the adults who support them to understand their natural strengths and talents. She lives in Park City, Utah.

ptpinc.org

To inquire about booking Dawna Markova and Angie McArthur for a speaking engagement, please contact the Penguin Random House Speakers Bureau.

speakers@penguinrandomhouse.com